THE LIBRARY

D0426148

WITHDRAWN

POST-COWBOY ECONOMICS

 Pay and Prosperity in the New American West

THOMAS MICHAEL POWER AND RICHARD N. BARRETT

ISLAND PRESS

Washington • Covelo • London

Copyright © 2001 by Island Press

All rights reserved under International and Pan-American Copyright Conventions. No part of this book may be reproduced in any form or by any means without permission in writing from the publisher: Island Press, 1718 Connecticut Ave., N.W., Suite 300, Washington, DC 20009.

Library of Congress Cataloging-in-Publication Data

Power, Thomas M.
  Post-cowboy economics : pay and prosperity in the new American west / Thomas Michael Power, Richard N. Barrett.
      p. cm.
Includes bibliographical references and index.
  ISBN 1-55963-820-6 — ISBN 1-55963-821-4
  1. West (U.S.)—Economic policy. 2. Income—West (U.S.) I. Barrett, Richard N. II. Title.
  HC107.A17 P69 2001
  338.978—dc21
                                    2001003027

British Library Cataloguing in Publication Data available.

Printed on recycled, acid-free paper ✺

Manufactured in the United States of America
10 9 8 7 6 5 4 3 2 1

We dedicate this book to the women
whose tolerance of our foibles and
whose support, even when we were lost
in obscure and abstract puzzles,
have allowed us to finish
many productive projects.
To our wives—
Sharon Barrett and Pamela Shore—
this book is gratefully dedicated.

Contents

List of Figures

List of Tables

Acknowledgments

This book began with a research project funded by the Liz Claiborne and Art Ortenberg Foundation. Both Liz Claiborne and Art Ortenberg have a deep personal commitment to Montana and the Mountain West. Their concern about the increasingly harsh and angry tone of public discourse during the mid-1990s led them to propose a study that would track the social and economic changes under way to see whether economic change might be contributing to this conflict. We enthusiastically agreed to do the economic analysis for Montana and put it in the context of the other states of the Mountain West. The working papers developed during the course of that research project form the core of this book. Our extended discussions, and sometimes debates, with Liz and Art and with Jim Murtaugh, the foundation's executive director, helped focus and tighten the analysis, but these individuals and the foundation, of course, have no responsibility for the final results of our research or this book.

Many of our colleagues at the University of Montana and in Montana state government also provided valuable assistance by reading drafts of chapters and helping us solve particular data problems. Doug Dalenberg, our colleague in the university's Department of Economics, read drafts of almost all the working papers and offered many valuable suggestions. Other researchers in the region, especially William Beyers and his graduate students, assisted us with critiques of the related papers we presented at annual meetings of the Pacific Northwest Regional Economic Conference. For help in editing and focusing our writing, we thank Len Broberg, Ron Erickson, Eban Goodstein, Ernie Niemi, Bob Ream, and Tom Roy. At the state capitol, Governor Marc Racicot helped us gain access to the unemployment insurance database and Phil Brooks in the Montana Department of Labor and Industry helped us with our data needs, and we thank them for their assistance. Of course, none of these individuals are responsible for our not always taking their advice.

Thomas Power would like to acknowledge the financial support he received over the years from the Charles Engelhard Foundation and The Brainerd Foundation for this and other writing projects. He also appreciates the Montana Human Rights Network's support of and interest in the economic issues discussed in this book.

The University of Montana, of course, supported us in our research efforts even when our results did not please some of those on whom the university relies for financial support. That is a tribute to the people of Montana, who insist on the need for their university's independence from powerful economic and political interests.

Finally, we want to thank Becky Hofstad, administrative assistant for the Department of Economics. With appropriately biting but good-natured humor, she helped control the chaos and manage our computer network so that we could go productively about our work.

Preface

During the 1980s and 1990s, the people of the Mountain West shared a particular, pessimistic understanding about how their economy worked, how it was
changing, and why it was failing. In this book we challenge that popular understanding and its implications and propose a new way of looking at the economy of the region.

GROWTH AND ANXIETY IN THE MOUNTAIN WEST

Since at least the 1970s, the American Mountain West—the region made up
of the states of Arizona, Colorado, Idaho, Montana, Nevada, New Mexico,
Utah, and Wyoming—has been in the thrall of sweeping economic, political,
and social change. In particular, once-important natural resource industries
have declined dramatically as sources of jobs and income. Since these industries—mining and metal processing, logging and lumber products, and agriculture—historically supported European settlement and are widely believed
still to be the economic lifeblood of the region's rural areas and small cities,
their decline has provoked deep economic anxiety: the fear that large parts of
the region will become depressed and its residents will be forced to move elsewhere. And because the federal government controls a significant part of the
Mountain West's natural landscapes and resources, federal government policies, especially those intended to protect the environment, are often blamed

for the decline of the natural resource sector and the economic collapse that is expected to follow.

But despite these fears, changing industrial structure has not triggered a decline in the region or an overall loss of jobs, income, or residents. On the contrary: as industrial transformation has proceeded, in-migration, employment, and aggregate real income (the total dollar income received by all residents, adjusted for inflation) have boomed. During the last half of the twentieth century, the Mountain West was the fastest-growing multi-state region of the United States. During this period, only one other region, the coastal states of the Pacific West, seriously challenged this lead, and during the 1990s the Mountain West grew twice as fast as this previously close competitor.[1]

This very visible economic vitality, however, has not put most leaders and residents at ease. They are certain that the declines in their historical natural resource "economic base" are damaging individuals, families, and communities. Despite ongoing growth in most of the region's non-metropolitan counties, as well as in its large cities, fear, anger, anxiety, and public conflict over natural resource policy have grown. Even as the region led the country in job creation, in-migration, and growth in production of goods and services, there were signs of economic distress—falling real pay, per capita income growth that lagged behind that of the United States as a whole, increased inequality, and persistently high poverty rates—that were taken as evidence of an economy in decline. As one regional commentator characterized it, the economic transformation to a post–natural resource economy was creating a "servant" economy: hidden by the glitter of the economic growth was the loss of family-wage, blue-collar jobs and the proliferation of low-paid "service" jobs.

This perceived decline in the economic well-being of most residents, especially those living in small cities and rural areas, has fueled harsh anti-environmental and anti-government movements. The federal government, through its environmental policies, is accused of waging a "war on the West" that is impoverishing the region's families and small communities by crippling the region's historical economic base. Anti-government activists and natural resource industry interests depict the Mountain West as a region in which natural resources provide the only high-wage jobs possible; in which the decline in natural resource industries has led to collapsing incomes, greater inequality, and persistent poverty as good, high-wage jobs have been replaced by low-wage jobs in services and trade; and in which natural resource production, and by extension the whole economy, has been strangled by restrictive environmental policies, particularly those of a federal government unresponsive to local needs.

COWBOY ECONOMICS

This book challenges all these beliefs. Analysis of evidence from a wide variety of sources and a more accurate depiction of how local and regional economies operate within the national economy allow us to provide a new interpretation of the economy of the Mountain West. We show that despite incomes that are low compared with those in the rest of the country, the region is not suffering from general impoverishment; the perception that the Mountain West is increasingly poor reflects a misunderstanding of how local labor markets work and of the choices people make in seeking to improve their well-being. And we show that environmental protection, rather than threatening economic well-being, enhances welfare and protects the very source of the economic vitality the Mountain West enjoys. Among other results, we show that the change in regional industrial structure—the decline of natural resource and other goods-producing industries and the growth of services and trade—has not damaged the regional economy. Far more pervasive national and international economic forces, however, have had a profound effect on the economies of the region.

This book focuses on how people think about the regional economy. We believe that most residents of the Mountain West and their political and business leaders share a conventional understanding of the region's economy that is at odds with the way a national market economy actually functions and influences the regional economies within it. This conventional economic wisdom is both pervasive and firmly entrenched. It is, however, primarily tied to the region's historical economic experience, not the present economic reality. For that reason, we label this way of looking at the local and regional economy *cowboy economics*. With this label, we draw on the dominant cultural symbol of the American West, the cowboy, to represent all the natural resource industries: ranching and farming, of course, but also mining and logging and the manufacturing activities associated with them.

With this phrase we mean no disrespect. The exploitation of natural resources has a history that stretches back to the beginnings of human society. As a species, we have been engaged in these activities longer than almost any other. They were the reason European Americans came to inhabit the Mountain West. American folklore is replete with stories praising the hard work, determination, and heroism of those who toiled in and on the earth: the mountain men, Paul Bunyan, the "little house on the prairie," and Joe Hill, in addition to the symbol that has lasted the longest and even spread to urban centers, the cowboy.

In contrast, as the title of this book makes clear, we offer what we think is a more accurate and contemporary analysis and interpretation of the economies of the Mountain West: a *post-cowboy* economics, an economics that recognizes the transformation of the economies of the region that began during the last half of the twentieth century and continues today.

ABOUT THE BOOK

In the chapters that follow, we explain what we believe are the factual flaws in the conventional belief that the Mountain West is being harmed by a decline in its historical natural resource base and related environmental restrictions on the exploitation of public lands and resources. We present a good deal of evidence for our position, in a variety of forms, which we hope patient readers will find compelling. One of our aims is to convince readers that fearful, crisis-driven environmental and economic development policies are unnecessary and inappropriate; there is time to consider what should be done and what will really serve the public interest. At the same time, we recognize the plight of many families and communities as they react to change or the fear that the economic rug is being jerked from underneath them. We have made every effort to understand their situation and respond to their needs.

In chapter 1, we lay out in some detail the conventional view of the Mountain West as a region in trouble. In chapters 2 and 3, we provide details of the remarkable changes in pay, income, and economic structure that have occurred in the Mountain West since the 1970s. In chapter 4, we present evidence on the relationship between change in industrial structure and the effect of that change on average pay and income. In chapter 5, we examine regional pay gaps in detail and investigate whether such gaps represent real economic losses to residents or are compensated for by regional differences in amenities and cost of living. In chapter 6, we critique the incomplete economic thinking that has led the Mountain West to misconstrue the transformation it has been undergoing. Given this critique, chapter 7 considers how economic development and other public economic policies might be redirected to better serve the public interest and the needs of the most vulnerable of the region's citizens. Finally, chapter 8 summarizes the results of our empirical and conceptual analysis.

NOTES

1. For historical state population levels, see U.S. Census Bureau 1999a.

Post-Cowboy
ECONOMICS

CHAPTER 1

 The View from
the Cowboy Economy

conomic and environmental policy debates in the Mountain West are
often, indeed almost always, conducted under a cloud of tension, anger,
and barely contained violence. Even minor local issues, which should
be easy to resolve, tend instead to escalate into major conflicts involving political activists, office holders, and federal employees from across the region.
Consider, for example, the case of the Jarbridge road.

ANGER AND REBELLION ON THE JARBRIDGE

In the spring of 1999, the USDA Forest Service closed a short stretch of a national
forest road along the Jarbridge River north of Elko, Nevada. The road, which
had recently been washed out by a flood, led to a popular local picnic spot and
a trailhead for the Jarbridge Wilderness, and the area's residents wanted it rebuilt
and access to these sites restored. But because the river was the southernmost
home of the endangered bull trout and rebuilding the road threatened to damage this important fish habitat, the Forest Service had instead opted for closure.

Residents of the area, who saw the closure as another federal government
effort to deny them access to public lands and resources, were outraged. In Octo-
ber of that year, a group of citizens, with the support of the county government
and led by a Nevada legislator, announced their intention to rebuild the road
on their own. When a federal court stopped the move, anger and resentment at
the Forest Service mushroomed.

Local citizens soon found additional official support. Representative Helen Chenoweth-Hage, a Republican from Idaho, one of the region's leading critics of both the federal government and the environmental movement, scheduled a special congressional hearing in Elko to investigate the Forest Service's actions.

Federal employees felt besieged. Gloria Flora, supervisor of the national forest in which the road was located, resigned rather than participate in the hearing, saying: "When a member of the United States Congress joins forces with [anti-government activists], using the power of the office to stage a public inquisition of federal employees . . . , I must protest. . . . I refuse to participate in this charade of normalcy" (*Missoulian* 1999). The strident anti-government rhetoric, she thought, had gotten out of hand, threatening the safety of the federal workers for whom she was responsible. In recent years in Nevada, two federal government office buildings and a vehicle had been blown up. As Flora later explained: "Rather than waiting for a bomb or for someone to get hurt, I decided the best thing was for me to step down. I knew that my resignation would bring the kind of attention a bomb would, except it was a lot less dangerous" (Jamison 2000b).

In the following months, outrage at the road closure blossomed as anti-federal "sagebrush rebels" organized an interconnected series of events and rallies stretching across the Mountain West. Among these rebels was Jim Hurst, owner of a lumber mill in northwestern Montana, who organized a protest of his own that he dubbed the "shovel brigade." He asked supporters to purchase shovels, sign them, and send them to him. He and as many others as he could recruit would deliver a hoped-for 10,000 shovels to a July 4 work party that would defy the federal courts and rebuild the Jarbridge road. Hurst said he was motivated by fear for the future of the traditional blue-collar, resource-based way of life in the Rocky Mountain West. "Something has to happen," he said, "or the West as we know it is going to be lost" (Devlin 2000b). He apparently found a sympathetic listener in Judy Martz, Montana's lieutenant governor, who signed and sent a shovel.[1]

Shovel brigade sympathizers held a variety of events in Montana to build support. A federal tax day rally was organized in Libby, in northwestern Montana, by, among others, a Montana state representative. The flyer announcing the event called for a "mass rally of civil disobedience against the Clinton environmental regime's war on the West," including "forceful civil disobedience. . . . No more negotiating; no more public meetings." A letter from the organizers, attached to the flyer, objected to "global governance" and the United Nations' purported attempt to take over the American West. "Wake up and smell the napalm, this won't be pretty," the organizers' letter warned. It also referred to "little Clintonista enviro-twerps" and asked whether the federal government and the United Nations intended to "starve or slaughter us." Organizers planned to burn the United Nations flag as part of the protest (Jamison 2000a).

Before the rally took place, local government officials, including law enforcement personnel, worried about the potential for both violence and damage to the city's reputation, pressed organizers to cancel it.

The shovel brigade, however, continued its organizing, energized by the proposal of President Bill Clinton's administration to set all remaining federal roadless areas off limits to logging. A caravan of logging trucks converged on the University of Montana in Missoula to protest the initiative, attack the writings of university professors on behalf of environmental protection, and rally support for the July 4 citizens' road-building effort along the Jarbridge River. Thousands attended the rally. The issue at stake, they were told, went far beyond a small road in Nevada or the timber found in roadless areas. As the head of the Montana Wood Products Association put it, "The issue is not whether to build roads in 43 million acres of roadless national forest. This is a rural community issue. The issue is our traditional way of life" (Devlin 2000a).

A crowd of about 500, much smaller than promoters expected, gathered at the Jarbridge on July 4 and partially opened the closed road. They faced no opposition from federal law enforcement officials and no one was arrested, although federal scientists monitored the effects of the roadwork on the river. If bull trout were killed, the Forest Service said, protest organizers would be subject to prosecution under the Endangered Species Act of 1973. Legal battles over the road continued into 2001.

The Jarbridge road conflict is typical of what passes for politics-as-usual in the Mountain West. Repeatedly, the public hears that the very future of the region and its communities are at risk because of environmental regulation. The economy and the resource base that supports it are being strangled by outside forces, environmentalists, the federal government, or all these, and as a result, workers and their families are being forced to abandon generations-old ways of life and their historical homes. If that is the case, it is not surprising that citizens are willing to contemplate extreme measures to fight back.

It is largely this widespread perception in the Mountain West of ongoing economic decline and community disruption, especially in rural areas, that energizes the fractious and uncivil politics. These economic fears have helped move the region significantly to the right politically, to the point of legitimizing what in the past would have been considered extreme and socially dangerous positions that no elected official would have supported.

These economic perceptions and fears are tied to a particular way of understanding the economy and public economic policy. In this book, we call this understanding "cowboy economics" because of both the nostalgic longing for a fading way of life that informs it and the natural resource–based economic prescription it yields.

ECONOMIC CONFUSION:
JUST WHERE IS THE REGION GOING?

During the 1990s, five of the country's ten fastest-growing states were in the Mountain West. Of the three that did not make it into the top ten, New Mexico was eleventh, Montana sixteenth, and Wyoming thirty-third (U.S. Census Bureau 1999b, table 28). This above-average regional population growth was primarily driven by net in-migration as people, voting with their feet, moved to the region in pursuit of what they perceived to be improved living situations. With population growth came a rapid expansion in jobs, real income, and overall economic activity. This growth was not limited to a few large metropolitan areas; the vast majority of the non-metropolitan counties in the region also grew rapidly.[2]

Despite this boom, however, a sense of unease, even insecurity, came to pervade public economic discourse. One important source of this economic anxiety was that over the previous three decades, real pay per job in all the region's states had stagnated or fallen while inequality of pay grew. To some extent, these developments mirrored what was happening throughout the country, where wages fell and inequality grew despite two sustained economic expansions and the attainment, by the end of the period, of record low unemployment rates. But in the Mountain West, the contrasts were sharper. Consider just the following:[3]

■ *Wages and salaries tumbled in the Mountain West, opening a significant gap in pay between its workers and other workers across the country.* Between 1978 and 1988, real pay per job fell by 10 percent across the Mountain West and by 20 percent in Montana. In the early 1970s, pay per job in both Montana and the rest of the region was only 5 percent below the national average; by 1998, the difference had grown to 11 percent for the region and 33 percent for Montana. Half of the states in the region (Montana, Wyoming, New Mexico, and Idaho) ranked among the lowest ten states in pay per job, with Montana dead last.

■ *As wages fell, inequality as measured by the gap between poor and well-to-do families grew significantly.* In the Mountain West in 1978–1980, the average income of families in the richest one-fifth of the population was seven times greater than that of families in the poorest one-fifth; by 1996–1998, it was ten times greater.[4]

■ *These adverse changes were not due to overall job loss or slow job growth.* On the contrary, from 1988 to 1998, total employment in the Mountain West grew by 42 percent, compared with 19 percent for the country as a whole. During the same period, population in the region grew by 26 percent, compared with 11 percent for the rest of the country.

■ *But as employment grew rapidly, the quality of the new jobs appeared suspect.* From 1969 to 1996, the number of workers in the Mountain West holding part-time jobs grew substantially. In 1969, Montanans, for example, worked an average of 38 hours per week, as did other American workers; by 1996, these hours had declined to 32 in Montana and 34.4 in the rest of the country (Montana Department of Labor and Industry 1999, p. 20).

■ *To make ends meet, more and more workers appeared to have to hold down more than one job.* In 1996, six of the eight states of the Mountain West had an above-average portion of their workforce holding multiple jobs. At 60 percent above the national average, Montana was the highest in the country. Idaho and Wyoming were in the top eight, with each state 50 percent above the national average (Bureau of Labor Statistics 1999b). For the Mountain West as a whole, the average number of jobs per worker increased by about one-third between 1978 and 1996.

Reading all these facts and figures in their local newspapers, or simply responding to their own experiences, many residents of the region came to believe that their economy was in serious trouble despite the rapid economic expansion. They reported that it was harder than ever for families to make ends meet, that two-earner families and persons holding multiple jobs were being worked to death, and that everybody was being taxed to the limit. Longtime residents believed that their grown children, particularly if they were well educated, were leaving home because they simply could not find suitable jobs. In Montana, it rankled residents that by some measures, the state had fallen to last place in the country. By the same measures, residents of Utah, Idaho, and New Mexico fared a little better but were still distressed to find their states among the ten poorest.

Another major source of economic anxiety was that along with these seemingly dismal developments in the labor market came rapid restructuring of the economy: a sea change in which the economies of the Mountain West moved from the production of goods (primarily natural resources) to the delivery of services. Economic growth in the region was fast enough to ensure more employment in almost every major industrial group except agriculture, but from 1969 to 1996 the *share* of total income from goods production fell significantly, from 31 percent to 18 percent. Non-goods-producing activities, including trade, finance, and transportation as well as a variety of professional, personal, and business services, filled the gap. Services alone—medical care, automobile repair, legal representation, and the like—grew particularly rapidly: earnings from services grew from 12 percent to 20 percent of total earnings over the period.

In some respects, the decline in the importance of goods production in the Mountain West mimicked events elsewhere in the country. But distinctively in the Mountain West, the decline was dominated by the shrinking importance of industries that extracted and processed natural resources: mining, primary metals processing, lumber and wood products, and agriculture. The combined share of these industries in total employment fell from 11 percent to less than 4 percent between 1969 and 1998. The region now had a post–natural resource economy that paralleled the post-industrial economy emerging elsewhere in the country.

To many citizens, this transformation appeared to be no less than the disintegration of the region's economic base. Given that employment in natural resource industries was shrinking at the same time average pay and relative incomes were deteriorating, it is not surprising that these two trends were firmly linked in many residents' minds as cause and consequence.

As the Mountain West led the country in a vigorous economic expansion that attracted millions of new residents and thousands of new businesses, its economy and economic well-being were perceived to be deteriorating. It did not make sense. If millions of people moved to the Mountain West because it was a superior place to live, work, and raise a family, how could it also be a place with a crumbling economic base and inferior economic rewards? Amid these conflicting economic perceptions and the resulting confusion, it should not be surprising that the public economic dialogue and resulting policy also became confused and misdirected.

COWBOY ECONOMICS: HOW THE REGIONAL ECONOMY IS CONVENTIONALLY UNDERSTOOD

In seeking to interpret the economic confusion around them, the people of the Mountain West arrived at a popular, but seriously flawed, understanding of how the regional economy operates. It was this understanding that informed the thinking of the Jarbidge road protestors and that we earlier labeled "cowboy economics": an economic worldview that is widely shared—by politicians, business reporters, editorial writers, voting citizens, and many others, including some professional economists—and that has a profound but misleading influence on public economic discourse. Central to this understanding of the economy and the policies and practices that flow from it are the critical concepts of the economic base, the economic structure, and worker immobility.

The Ever Impending Economic Collapse

Until late in the twentieth century, economic activities centered on natural resources sustained the Mountain West's rural and small urban economies and shaped the region's political, social, and cultural identity. The symbols that identified this region in the minds of its residents—and most other Americans—were its unique landscapes and the livelihoods those landscapes supported. On the high plains and plateaus, hardy men and women came to ranch and to create the cowboy culture that grew up around their hardscrabble lives. In the mountains, miners flocked to the gold rush communities that would later become ghost towns, and independent prospectors—"sourdoughs" and their trusty mules—explored the remote but promising backcountry. On the shoulders of the mountains and along creeks with northern and eastern exposures, there was timber to be harvested and milled. In the broad river valleys, farmers made a good living from lush crops raised on irrigated land.

It was taken for granted, of course, that the region's entire economy relied on these natural resource industries. If the flow of income to mines or logging camps or farms or ranches were interrupted, other businesses—banks, blacksmiths, general stores, schools, the offices of doctors and lawyers, newspapers—would soon wither and die. This understanding came to be formalized in the export base model of the economy, according to which the region was linked to the national economy mainly through markets for the natural resource–based products it could export.[5] Such export industries generated a flow of income that, when spent, became the source of sales and employment in trade, services, and other locally oriented economic activities. If this flow of export revenue were to falter, sales and income all across the regional economy would fall. In the export base model, the key role of natural resource industries was to stimulate demand for economic activity throughout the local economy.

This assumed reliance on natural resource industries made the economies of the Mountain West especially vulnerable to federal public land management and environmental policies. More than 25 percent of Montana and almost 80 percent of Nevada are federally owned. For the other states of the Mountain West, federal ownership lies between these two extremes (U.S. Census Bureau 1999b, table 394). Because the activities of natural resource industries involve significant manipulation of natural landscapes, their environmental effects have come under increasing scrutiny, especially when they operate on public lands. The result has been increased government regulation of these industries and reductions in the intensity with which public landscapes are used for commercial purposes. Because of environmental concerns, the Forest Service has reduced the level of timber harvest in national forests and raised the cost of what harvest it does allow. The U.S. Bureau of Land Management is under increasing pressure to reduce the level of livestock grazing on public lands. Each new mineral development proposal brings controversy and opposition that have significantly increased the cost of getting a mining project approved. The federal government has largely cut off the flow of funds to support irrigated agriculture and is under pressure to breach or remove dams in order to reverse the environmental damage associated with past federal water projects.

According to the export base model, hard times in the natural resource industries can be expected to cascade through the economy, and in fact declines in these basic industries have often led to projections of economic catastrophe across the region. For instance, concerns about the adequacy of habitat for several endangered species, including the northern spotted owl, grizzly bear, salmon, and bull trout, led to major reductions in federal timber harvests in the Pacific Northwest, including Idaho and Montana. Timber interest groups predicted that reduced access to federal timber would turn the region into a "new Appalachia," with more than 100,000 jobs lost, most of them located in remote small towns and rural areas. In the logging towns of central Idaho, six of nine mills were projected to close, causing the number of jobs in some towns to fall by three-fourths and pay per worker to fall by one-quarter to one-third (Robison, McKetta, and Peterson 1996). Across the Mountain West, other natural resource users and government agencies predicted similar dire consequences for the closing of mines, shutting down of smelters, reduction in public land grazing, and loss of water for irrigation and generation of electricity.

Fortunately for the region, these catastrophic consequences never materialized; the Mountain West was not driven into depression as its historical economic base contracted. Quite the contrary: the region experienced an ongoing employment and population boom. In the nineteenth century, the opportunity to exploit the Mountain West's land, forests, and minerals triggered the rush of population that settled the region. One hundred years later, a new rush was "resettling" the region as natural resource industries steadily declined.

Economic Structure and Earnings:
A New Role for Natural Resource Industries

That employment and population could grow despite stagnation of the traditional natural resource base suggests that natural resource industries are no longer the engines of regional economic growth they once were. Many residents and leaders in the region believe, however, that those industries still play a critical structural role in the economy, particularly in determining individual pay and household income.

With no help from farms or ranches or mines or forests, the economy may have proved itself capable of generating lots of new jobs in trade and services. But what kinds of jobs were they? If pay and benefits measure job quality, the jobs that were lost in natural resource industries were good, whereas the jobs gained in trade and services were assumed to be bad. Skilled and experienced workers, moving from mines and mills to malls or cafés or ski areas, apparently have seen their wages plummet and fear that their children, entering the labor market for the first time, will never enjoy the opportunities they had. Structural change has, in this view, driven down average pay and degraded labor market opportunities. Natural resource industries may no longer drive the economy forward, but they are seen as the last best hope for a decent job, and their high wages are thought to bolster the overall economy.

The sense of insecurity engendered by structural change in the economy has other dimensions. The new economy emerging in the Mountain West does provide many good, well-paid jobs, particularly in professional service industries such as health care. But middle-aged workers leaving the mines or forests cannot take up heart surgery; nor, armed with high school diplomas, do their children. They believe that it is affluent newcomers who get the good jobs while the economic prospects of longtime residents decline dramatically despite the booming economy. Some are hard pressed enough to pick up and leave.

It is not the prospect of diminished opportunity alone that makes structural change disquieting. Moving from working the mines to working the mall means more than just a pay cut. It means a loss of touch with what made living and working in the region different—a dulling of the sense of place.

The image of skilled workers forced to take trivial, poorly paid jobs is a compelling one, and it resonates in public discussions of the Mountain West economy. In the following chapters, we explore the accuracy of this widely shared image of what the transformation of the Mountain West economies has meant to the region's workers: were workers forced out of highly paid and skilled natural resources employment into flipping burgers, washing cars, and cleaning toilets for the minimum wage?

Good Jobs, Bad Jobs, and Captive Workers

For the structural explanation of low and falling wages to make sense, its proponents must make certain assumptions. These concern the way in which various markets in the Mountain West are linked to their counterparts in the rest of the country or even the world.

In the case of products of various kinds, these linkages are taken to be tight indeed. The profitability and survival of producers of lumber products or minerals or biotechnology research depend on production costs, of course, but also critically on prices in national markets and the cost of the transportation giving access to those markets.

But comparable external influences from national market forces are not thought to affect local labor markets, where wages and incomes are assumed to be determined. If wages in the Mountain West are collapsing relative to those in the rest of the country because good job offers are disappearing, it must be that workers are captive in the region. Otherwise, they could leave and earn national-scale wages somewhere else. For the growing wage gap between western workers and their counterparts elsewhere in the country to be structural, then, requires a labor force with low mobility and an isolated, rather than nationally integrated, labor market.

If workers are immobilized in this way, what individual workers earn will not be very well correlated with their productive characteristics—their education, skill, experience, and the like. Rather, their earnings will depend substantially, though not exclusively, on the jobs they are lucky or unlucky enough to get. In accounting for earnings differences, it is more important to know something about the characteristics of the workers' actual jobs than about the workers' individual qualifications.

A number of factors may determine whether a particular job is well paid or not, but for people focused on the structural change in the Mountain West economies, one of the most important factors is the industry in which the job is located. A substantial body of research has confirmed that some industries tend to pay higher wages than others for workers with the same qualifications and doing the same type of job. Moreover, industries that pay higher wages in one occupation tend to do so for all occupations. Thus, for example, electricians tend to earn more in the mining industry than in retail trade, and so do clerks, security guards, personnel managers, and most other workers. Whether industry is more important than personal characteristics such as education, training, and occupation in determining individual income is a critical question, but if the root of low pay is structural, industry must be assumed to be important indeed.

Solving the Problem:
The Structural View of Economic Development Policy

The low earnings and income that are the source of much economic anxiety in the Mountain West are broadly understood to have structural origins. This means that the industrial structure of the economy is bottom-heavy with activities, such as retail trade, that provide bad, poorly paid jobs and that it lacks activities that offer good, well-paid ones. Given this diagnosis, the cure for the low-wage problem becomes obvious: change the structure of employment opportunities. But how is that to be done?

The appropriate strategy is simple, although hard to implement: identify potential high-wage industries; find out what they would need from the local community to get them to shift some of their activities to this particular location; and then give them what they want, be it tax breaks, reductions in environmental regulation, or a labor market unfettered by collective bargaining. In addition, although the region's historical economic base probably cannot be rebuilt entirely, its remaining natural resource jobs should be zealously protected as part of the new economic mix. Because keeping existing high-wage jobs is easier than recruiting new ones, state and local governments may urge federal natural resource management agencies to increase access to resources on public lands or to relax existing environmental regulations. Another element of the conventional strategy is to increase the demand for labor across the board, on the supposition that local wages will rise and low-income family members will enter the paid workforce.

For other "new economy" development advocates in the Mountain West, however, the structural problem and its solution are both more comprehensive and more complex. Providing high-wage jobs requires stimulating the growth, within the region, of industries that are prospering in a dynamic and changeable national and world economy. High-wage jobs are to be found in biotechnology, e-commerce, high-technology manufacturing, software development, and professional services. This economic development strategy looks forward to new opportunities rather than backward to the historical economic base, but it keeps its focus on the structure of the local economy.

Governments have devised a number of ways to promote the growth of these types of industries: selective financial inducements and recruitment strategies, industrial and technology parks, cooperative university research programs, publicly supported marketing, targeted tax cuts, and locational promotions emphasizing quality-of-life advantages for potential employers. In many instances, such strategies can be reinforced by the maintenance of high environmental quality, and proponents of these strategies often oppose the cruder attacks of natural resource industries on environmental regulations. But ironically, even ardent environmentalists share with the natural resource industries the conviction that the cause of low wages is structural and that the most pressing need is for good, high-wage jobs.

The structural view of local Mountain West economies is widely accepted by residents. To understand their local economies, westerners resort not only to economic theory but also to their history, to culture, and to metaphor. They appear to think of their economy as though it were that of a ranch family on the high plains a century ago: self-reliant, working hard, tied to the land, plowing savings back into their ranch, producing whatever will sell in distant and uncontrollable markets, accepting whatever income those markets will bestow, and when times get tough, taking in paying guests. However economically useful— or irrelevant—this metaphor might be today, it has great cultural appeal. It represents the economy of the region's history and identity, the economy of cowboys, miners, homesteaders, and loggers, the economy of the Old West. The cultural appeal of this economic metaphor may, however, be distracting westerners and preventing them from seeing and managing a quite different current economic reality.

EXPLOITING PUBLIC ANXIETY: THE POLITICAL CONSEQUENCES OF CONFUSED ECONOMICS

The way people think about the economy matters. It colors what they see and the way they design policies to promote the public's economic well-being. Conventional beliefs about how the regional economy operates, built as they are on assumptions of an immobile workforce and the dominance of local industrial structure in determining local economic well-being, guide the public economic discourse in particular directions.[6]

The evident economic vitality of the Mountain West might have been expected to produce a positive and optimistic social and political climate, with the ready availability of jobs and other economic opportunities reducing economic anxiety and insecurity. But as the boom spread from the late 1980s through the entire decade of the 1990s and continued into the next century, local economic conflicts over environmental issues have gained in political importance instead of being muted by the region's economic successes. Opposition to environmental protection has repeatedly fed on, and in turn fed, economic anxiety, insecurity, and conflict. Despite an economic expansion that has lasted for more than a decade, many in the Mountain West continue to perceive environmental protection as an economic threat.

In western Montana, for instance, the wood products industry led an effort to convince local government officials and citizens that the federal Interior Columbia Basin Ecosystem Management Project represented a threat to the region's economic survival. Playing off the title of Hillary Rodham Clinton's book *It Takes a Village,* a timber industry representative asserted, "They [the federal government and environmentalists] are taking your villages."[7] Elsewhere in

Montana, mining interests succeeded in lowering state water quality standards and fighting off a citizens' initiative to reinstate them. Legal battles continue over a citizen-passed initiative to ban the use of cyanide in gold mining and court rulings requiring the refilling of open pit mines.

In southern Utah, anger and resentment over the establishment of Grand Staircase–Escalante National Monument continues to dominate public dialogue. In Escalante itself, local government and business leaders who sought to accept the monument as a fait accompli and make the best of the new economic opportunities the monument could provide were driven out of office. Harassment of the few active environmentalists in the area has escalated toward violence. Meanwhile, the larger debate over wilderness protection in southern Utah is locked in a divisive stalemate.

Federal employees have become lightning rods in the storm of opposition to federal environmental policies. In Nevada, as mentioned at the beginning of this chapter, the supervisor of the American West's largest national forest resigned to protest what she saw as an unworkably hostile and threatening social and political climate for federal workers. The "county ordinance" movement, which originated in rural Catron County, New Mexico, and asserts that county governments can preempt federal land managers, has spread to much of the rural West and led to confrontations in Nevada, Utah, Idaho, and Wyoming. Individual vigilantes across the Mountain West have threatened federal land managers, even resorting at times to bombing or burning their offices.

All of the state governments surrounding Yellowstone National Park have refused to cooperate in the reintroduction of wolves there. Wyoming livestock interests have sued, with some preliminary success, to force the federal government to remove those wolves. In Montana, the state government will not allow federal wildlife agency personnel to use road-killed deer to feed orphaned wolf pups.

Conflict over environmental policies often centers on small rural communities that are particularly resource dependent, but ongoing economic insecurity and social tension have influenced electoral politics all across the region. Candidates for virtually every state, federal, and local office appear compelled to recognize the seriousness of the economic crisis, the vital importance of "good new jobs," and the need to strike a cautious "balance" between environmental protection and economic growth. Voting patterns have become markedly more conservative, with increasing Republican domination of congressional delegations, governorships and legislatures, and local governments. States that once elected politicians with impressive environmental records, such Cecil Andrus and Frank Church of Idaho or Mike Mansfield and Lee Metcalf of Montana, have sent to Washington harsh critics of federal environmental and resource policies such as Helen Chenoweth-Hage, Larry Craig, Ron Marlenee, and Conrad Burns. Both Idaho and Utah have become one-party states with nary a Democrat in sight and nearly the entire political establishment committed to an industrialized "working landscape." In Utah, the political establishment launched a vigorous anti-wilderness campaign despite broad public support for designation of expansive new wilderness areas in the state.

The most disturbing symptom of increased social conflict within the region has been the rise of groups that mix particularly virulent anti-government sentiments with appalling bigotry and hate. Armed strongholds of white supremacist groups have developed in the northern Idaho panhandle, and their members have been linked to violence in both the Pacific Northwest and southern California. Members of militia-type organizations have threatened the lives of local government officials across Montana while engaging in massive financial fraud. One group held agents of the Federal Bureau of Investigation at bay in central Montana for many weeks. The anti-Christian, anti-Semitic, white supremacist World Church of the Creator, whose members have gone on killing sprees elsewhere in the country, holds its national meetings in a small town outside Missoula, Montana.[8]

It is not just psychopaths and social outcasts who have embraced the ideas espoused by these groups. Many elected officials in the Mountain West have openly sided with and defended them as well. Legislation they support gets hearings at which critics are hissed and booed into silence. County commissioners challenge federal regulations and public ownership of western lands by bulldozing roads into protected roadless areas. State and local officials openly encourage violation of the Endangered Species Act by supporting local citizens who "shoot, shovel, and shut up."

Why right-wing groups flourish in the Mountain West is a complex issue, but Ed Marston, longtime observer of the region and publisher of the regional newspaper *High Country News,* has linked anti-environmental and generally reactionary politics to low and falling pay in the following terms (Marston 1999):

> I believe the nonmetropolitan West . . . is [economically] unstable, and that that instability shows up in our politics. From across the [Mountain West], we send people to Washington, D.C., who are like the politicians of the pre-1960s South: They hate the federal government, they practice the politics of resentment, and they have no vision of the future other than to continue to run for office by being for guns and against environmental protection.
>
> If the nonmetropolitan West were healthy, it would not be so reactive. We would think in terms of the land, of education, of libraries and of conservation. If

we were satisfied with our lots, we would not be presiding over the reckless transformation of the region.

What is the answer? I see a middle-class society, with middle-class aspirations, as the best way to protect and nurture the West. Such a society requires good wages, on a par with national wages. What we then do with the wages will become the next fight. But we need the wages.

Mountain West state and local government leaders have also identified low pay as the most crucial problem the region faces. Divergent trends in economic growth and real pay led the Western Regional Conference of the Council of State Governments to commission a 1995 report whose very title expresses the concern: *The West on a Slippery Slope: High Growth, Low Pay.* The report summarized its findings as follows (Grose 1995, p. vii):

Throughout modern memory the West has been seen as a region of growth and opportunity. More people came, new jobs were created, homes were built, land was developed, schools, roads and hospitals were constructed. It has all presented a picture of growing wealth as well as increased growth. But [this report] has identified some serious, long term and systemic flaws in this picture. . . . It is clear that in most western states since the mid 1970s, the quality of economic growth, as measured by personal income per capita, average household income, or wage earner income, has declined in a relative sense.

To quote Marston (1996) again, low pay and income are the "warts" on the superficially glittering "New West" economies. The loss of jobs in natural resource industries has evidently left the region without culturally meaningful or economically rewarding work. The economy of the rancher, miner, and logger is seen as giving way to a "servant economy" in which residents engage in demeaning, low-paid work at the behest of well-heeled visitors.

If this is the reality, it is no wonder that many residents are hostile to these economic changes and that the hostility at times boils over into scapegoating, bigotry, and violence. Economic anxiety and the sense of victimization that arise out of the region's rapid structural change, even when moderated, support public policies that undermine environmental protection and allow important public services to deteriorate. Whether this is an appropriate or productive response is the subject of later chapters. It is clear, however, that the economic anxiety, fear, and anger are real. But in order to do something effective about them, residents of the Mountain West have to understand what has actually been happening to their economy. Confused perceptions and the emotions they evoke are not reliable guides to good public economic policy.

CHALLENGING THE STRUCTURAL INTERPRETATION: POST-COWBOY ECONOMICS

In this book, we challenge the conviction that the economies of the Mountain West have been impoverished by changes in industrial structure. We suspect that the roots of low wages and low income lie elsewhere, and that in failing to recognize this fact, even the best-intentioned policy makers will take steps that lead either nowhere or in the wrong direction.

Throughout the following chapters, we test the validity of cowboy economics by holding it up against the facts. Where the theory and the facts do not fit, we provide what we believe are more compelling explanations for what is happening, a sounder understanding of why and how the environment matters, and a clear account of the nature of the public's interest in economic development.

Testing the Structural Hypothesis

Proving that the decline of natural resource industries and the shift of jobs to services caused wages to fall and inequality to grow in the Mountain West may appear to be deceptively simple. After all, were these events not closely associated with each other? Did all these changes not happen largely at the same time? Indeed they did. But were these events linked causally or through mere coincidence? Was the changing structure of the region really the cause of its declining earnings?

In chapter 4, we approach this matter by asking what would have happened to average pay if there had been *no* shift in employment from high- to low-wage industries.

But averages, of course, do not tell the stories of individuals, so we also present an analysis of the wage histories of hundreds of thousands of workers as they moved from job to job over almost a decade. These histories can tell us how workers who left high-paid jobs in natural resource industries fared and whether they were forced into low-paid employment in retail trade and services. We also explore evidence about whether it was personal characteristics of individual workers or characteristics of the industries in which they happened to work that were most important in determining their earnings.

Alternatives to a Structural Interpretation

To reject the structural explanation of the changes that have taken place in the Mountain West, it is not enough to simply show that the theory does not fit the facts as well as one might like. Rather, it is important to formulate plausible alternative explanations that are even better supported by the factual evidence. It is, therefore, reasonable to ask what other explanations there might be for the decline in real pay and relative incomes in the Mountain West. We do this in chapter 5.

The leading alternative hypothesis is that pay and income in the Mountain West have largely followed trends established in the national economy and imported into the region by the free flow of people, capital, and workers. In short, the Mountain West is part of the national labor market, not an economic island unto itself. This hypothesis, of course, contradicts the popular assumption that the health of the Mountain West's economy is largely determined by the region's distinctive landscapes and natural resources, that the region is "a little ranch on the prairie" operating largely on a self-sufficient basis, exploiting the resources the natural landscape makes available.

This alternative to the structural hypothesis has an obvious flaw. If the region's wages are linked to wages in the rest of the country by national economic forces, how can it also be true that they are well below the national average? One possible answer lies in the fact that in making decisions about moving from place to place and job to job, families look not just at money wages but at the "whole package": wages, of course, but also cost of living, quality of schools, environmental amenities, personal security, recreational opportunities, taxes, and so forth. Even if wages are low compared with those in the rest of the country, workers may stay in or even move to the region if other elements in the package make up for the difference. If the shortfall gets too big, however, people will begin to leave. If it gets small enough, they will move in. This means that wages in the Mountain West will be linked to, but lower than, wages elsewhere. National labor markets prevail, but they work to establish different wage levels in different areas.

Ironically, under this hypothesis, it is the region's relative attractiveness—the curse of being the "last best place"—that gluts the labor market and depresses earnings.

Why and How the Environment Matters
In advancing a competing explanation of events in the Mountain West, we hope to promote a sounder understanding of why and how the environment matters in the economic life of the region.

If differences in amenities and the cost of living might explain differences in earnings from one place to another, then an important corollary is that even though they earn less, residents of the Mountain West may not be worse off than other Americans; what they lose in wages they may make back in lower living costs and better social and natural environments. Put another way, by their decision to live and work there, even though it means sacrificing money income, people in the region are making it clear that a high-quality environment enhances their well-being.

Within the context of this non-structural hypothesis, the public interest in the health of natural resource industries and in the policies by which they are regulated lies not in the creation of good jobs but in the provision of public amenities. The economic significance of opening new mines or protecting wilderness, for example, has less to do with the kinds of jobs that result than with the social and environmental amenities created or destroyed in the process. In contrast to what the structural hypothesis suggests, within this alternative view, allowing the environment to be degraded in the name of natural resource or other "good job" development might raise wages, but not because of good new jobs in mines or forests or mills. Rather, wages would rise because only better pay could attract workers to a region where destructive development reduces the quality of life.

Confusing Public and Private Interests

Should we blithely dismiss the economic problems of the region? After all, if wages are low because amenities are high, there seems to be nothing to worry about. And if wages have gone down because they were tracking falling wages all over America, not much can be done about it.

Such optimism and passivity would be wrong: the significant economic problems of the region, the anxieties they engender, and the efforts that state and local governments have made to solve them are real and significant. Too often, though, the problems are misunderstood, the anxieties are misplaced, and the efforts of government are ineffective or even counterproductive.

An important guide for economic policy makers is that their actions should clearly serve the public interest, not private interests alone. Distinguishing between the two is not always easy, but broadly speaking, serving the public interest means securing benefits of one sort or another that can be had only through collective action.

Economic development has both quantitative and qualitative dimensions. Quantitatively, development entails a growing economy with expanding population, employment, and money income along with a higher dollar volume of business activity. Qualitatively, it leads to rising standards of living for a region's residents. This may take the form of higher money incomes, but it also includes improvements in public services and environmental and social amenities and a growing social consensus that the economy provides a just and ample range of opportunities to its citizens.

Although the pursuit of qualitative development seems pretty clearly to be in the public interest, the same is not true of quantitative growth; bigger is not necessarily better. Larger communities do provide benefits to their residents: more diverse employment opportunities; a greater sense of commercial vitality, variety, and stability; and more support for community institutions such as churches, museums, and athletic leagues. But with these benefits come costs: congestion, loss of open space, loosened community ties, and the disappearance of small-town amenities. As a result, the overall effect of quantitative growth on well-being is, at best, ambiguous. To unambiguously serve the public interest, local economic development policies must raise the living standards, including both pay and the value of local amenities, of an area's *current* residents and not just provide opportunities for in-migrating newcomers. Policies that simply increase the size of the local economy may or may not be in the public interest.

When they contemplate what has happened to their earnings since the 1970s or the low rung they occupy on the nation's economic ladder, residents of the Mountain West may be legitimately concerned. Most people, after all, would like to see themselves and their neighbors and friends doing better, and the public interest would certainly be served if that could be brought about. But this concern and the urge to do something about it should be tempered by the facts that low earnings are compensated for by amenities other Americans do not enjoy and that local control over wages determined in national labor markets may be quite tenuous.

The distress that people express about the state of the economy, however, has roots far deeper than concern about their own standard of living; they extend to the realization that many of their neighbors have been mauled by the economic changes of the 1980s and 1990s. Even though real living standards in the region may not have fallen much *compared with* those in the rest of the country, they have, *along with* those in the rest of the country, fallen a good deal. In this respect, the decline in *average* earnings, as impressive and alarming as it is, disguises the fact that hardly anybody is really average. Unlike the children of Garrison Keillor's Lake Wobegone, some families do worse, even a lot worse, than average, and others, of course, do better. And the persistence of poverty and the growth in inequality tell us that it is disproportionately the poor who have done worse and the affluent who have done better. We believe that it is a profound and justifiable sense of economic disenfranchisement that fuels the politics of resentment and hostility that have emerged in the Mountain West.

As a response to this concern, economic development policies that simply promote quantitative growth will not do the trick. To serve the public interest, development policies must not just raise incomes or generate healthy-looking booms in business activity. They must also provide opportunity and economic justice to those in greatest need. In this respect, we believe, typical economic development policies, based as they often are on quantitative boosterism, will fail.

In the following chapters, we explore in some detail the conventional assumption that the economies of the Mountain West have been impoverished by the changes in industrial structure since the 1970s. We draw on research using many different sources of data that we analyzed with a variety of techniques. Some issues inevitably lie beyond the reach of the data. But we believe that in the following chapters, we present compelling evidence that the conventional understanding of the economies of the Mountain West is seriously flawed and that policies growing out of that understanding will fail. We go on to try to explain what *is* happening and what *will* work.

NOTES

1. Martz was elected governor of Montana in November 2000.
2. The exception to this pattern of non-metropolitan growth in the Mountain West was the Great Plains regions of Montana, Wyoming, and Colorado. Those areas shared the economic problems of the other Great Plains states rather than the economic growth that characterized the Mountain West.
3. Unless otherwise noted, all figures and statistics mentioned in the text throughout this book were computed by the authors using data from the Regional Economic Information System database (Bureau of Economic Analysis 1999). For a description of this data set, see the appendix.
4. We computed these ratios for the region as the state population weighted average of the eight state ratios listed in Bernstein et al. 2000, pt. 2, table 3, p. 11.
5. For a more detailed exposition of the export base model, see Shaffer 1989, pp. 28–34.
6. The politics of environmental regulation and natural resource management (and the economic understandings that inform those politics) are, of course, extremely contentious. In this section, we only scratch the surface. For two diametrically opposed and more expansive views, see Pendley 1995 and Echeverria and Eby 1995.
7. The phrase was used by Cary Hegreberg of the Montana Wood Products Association in various public forums; to our knowledge, it has not appeared in print.
8. Ken Toole (1997) argues that extreme right-wing organizations have flourished to the extent they have by appropriating and trading on more conventional conservative positions, such as opposition to government, especially gun control, and defense of private property. Their appeal, in other words, is not confined to a small and dysfunctional segment of an otherwise indifferent public. Toole is a Montana state senator and the founder and current executive director of the Montana Human Rights Network.

CHAPTER 2

Economic Deterioration amid Rapid Economic Growth?

Trends in Pay and Income in the Mountain West

Many economic concepts, even very important ones, can be hard to define and harder still to measure. Consider, for example, a concept that is central to this book: worker *well-being*. Most readers will have some notion of what worker well-being is. Some may even have an idea of how it is to be measured. But it turns out that the problem is not simple; exactly what it is that makes workers better off is not so obvious. And there are several competing measures of well-being that do not even necessarily tell the same story.

Take the case of a woman who worked in Montana between 1982 and 1998. If we assume that trends in average pay per job during this period paint an accurate picture of her personal experience at the time, we can conclude that her real annual pay would have declined by about $2,000, from $24,000 to $22,000. Taking the same approach, we find that a typical worker elsewhere in America would have seen her real pay rise by $4,000, from $29,000 to $33,000. Not only would the Montana worker have suffered an actual decline in the purchasing power of her pay, but also an $11,000 gap, fully 50 percent of the Montana worker's pay, would have developed between her pay and that of her fellow workers elsewhere in the country. It would not be surprising to conclude from these measures that the well-being of Montana workers and families had been compromised and that they had been left behind by the rest of the nation.

If, on the other hand, we characterize the economic well-being of Montanans using per capita income, we find that over the same time period, the real income of Montanans rose from $18,000 to $21,200. For a family of four, the real purchasing power of family income rose by $12,800 per year. For almost any family, that would have been a significant and welcomed improvement in economic well-being. Thus, using two quite plausible but competing measures of well-being, we arrive at contradictory conclusions regarding what happened to Montanans over the last two decades of the twentieth century.

Another example: over that same period, rapid job growth in the Mountain West was partially facilitated by the proliferation of part-time jobs, which supplanted the traditional full-time jobs with which a single worker could support a family. This trend was seen as a sign of labor market decay; it seemed to indicate clearly that workers could not earn enough and that economic well-being in the Mountain West was seriously deteriorating despite rapid expansion in employment opportunities.

But if we turn our attention from jobs to workers, we find that the data do not support the conclusion that there was not enough work to satisfy people. On the contrary: the average workweek of individuals has been remarkably stable for many decades. Moreover, there is a good deal of survey evidence that the vast majority of people who work part-time do so by choice. These facts suggest that employment opportunities available to support workers' economic objectives not only are not deteriorating but may, in fact, be improving. Again, different measures support two dramatically different interpretations of how well the economy has been performing.

This chapter explores these income and pay puzzles by analyzing more closely exactly how income and pay are measured and what each of these measures can tell us about the well-being of workers and families.

FALLING PAY AND INCOME: AN OVERVIEW

Nothing appears to signal an economic crisis in the Mountain West more starkly than the behavior of individual pay and income. In the mid-1990s, for example, real pay per job in the region was about $3,400, or 11 percent, less than it had been in 1978. At the same time, per capita real income in the Mountain West was about 90 percent of the national average, down from approximately 95 percent two decades earlier. In other words, what a worker could purchase with the earnings from a typical job had fallen, and to add insult to injury, the region had apparently been bypassed by the record expansion of the national economy in the 1990s.

The situation in just a few years, of course, does not tell the whole story, so in figures 2.1 and 2.2 we plotted earnings per job and income per capita for all the years from 1978 to 1998 for the United States as a whole, the country's

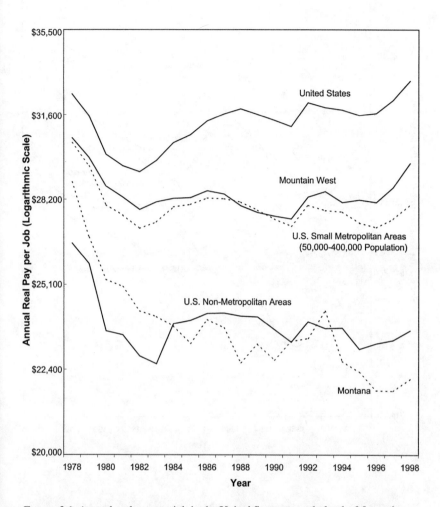

FIGURE 2.1. Annual real pay per job in the United States as a whole, the Mountain West, U.S. small metropolitan areas, U.S. non-metropolitan areas, and Montana, 1978–1998 (1998 dollars). Pay is plotted on a logarithmic scale; slopes of pay lines measure *rate* of change. *Source:* Bureau of Economic Analysis 1999.

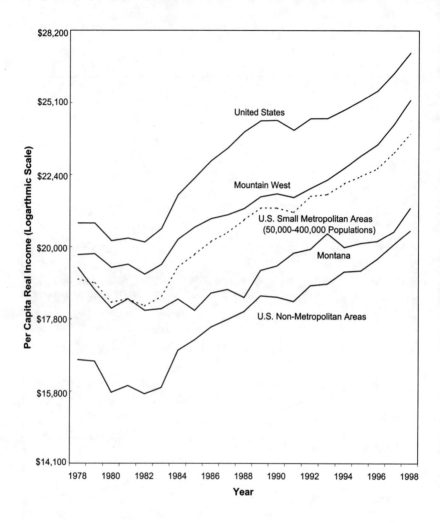

FIGURE 2.2. Per capita real income in the United States as a whole, the Mountain West, U.S. small metropolitan areas, U.S. non-metropolitan areas, and Montana, 1978–1998 (1998 dollars). Income is plotted on a logarithmic scale; slopes of income lines measure *rate* of change. *Source:* Bureau of Economic Analysis 1999.

small metropolitan and non-metropolitan areas, the Mountain West region as a whole, and Montana alone (the "worst case" in the region). We adjusted the vertical axes of these figures so that the slopes of the lines show the rate at which earnings and income changed in percentage terms. Where two lines in these figures converge, the percentage (or relative) difference between them was shrinking; where they diverge, the percentage difference was increasing.

For reasons we will explain later, earnings per job and income per capita tend to behave similarly but not identically. Figures 2.1 and 2.2 display some of these similarities and differences, and they also reveal several important facts about the behavior of both measures during the period 1978–1998:

- Early in the 1980s, when the United States economy entered the most severe recession since the Great Depression, both real earnings per job and income per capita fell in all areas of the country.
- With recovery from the recession after 1982, real income per capita in the country began a sustained rise. The same was true of the Mountain West, albeit at a slower pace. If real income per capita measures the standard of living,[1] residents of the region were becoming better off, but not relative to people in the rest of the country. This relative decline is one that residents tend to dwell on, and it is important to understand that it ended in 1988; after that, there was a partial recovery in relative income.
- For the country as a whole, real pay per job also began to rise after 1982, and by 1998 it was a little higher than it had been in 1978. The same was not true in the Mountain West, where after 1982, real earnings per job were virtually unchanged until 1997, when they began to rise. Relative to the rest of the country, real earnings per job in the region fell between 1982 and 1998.
- In both small and non-metropolitan areas in the rest of the country, trends in earnings and income were very much like those in the Mountain West. This means that these areas were subject to the same declines in earnings and income relative to the rest of the country. This fact is important, and we discuss its implications in detail in chapter 5.
- The experiences of the Mountain West states were not identical. Montana, in particular, showed the largest declines in pay per job and relative income, and during the 1990s the path of real earnings per job, though erratic, tended to slope down.

Table 2.1 summarizes, for the United States as a whole, for the Mountain West, and by state within the Mountain West, changes in real pay per job and

Table 2.1. Deterioration of Real Pay per Job and Relative per Capita Income in the Mountain West, 1978–1988 (1998 Dollars)

State/Region	1978–1988 Change		Difference in Growth in Average Pay and Income between State and U.S., 1978–1988		1998 Gap Relative to U.S.	
	Pay per Job	Per Capita Income	Pay per Job	Per Capita Income	Pay per Job	Per Capita Income
Mountain West	–$2,694	$1,512	–$2,044	–$1,739	–$3,491	–$1,980
U.S.	–$650	$3,251	—	—	—	—
Arizona	–$2,064	$2,798	–$1,414	–$453	–$2,814	–$2,997
Colorado	–$1,750	$2,469	–$1,100	–$783	–$146	$2,791
Idaho	–$2,654	$370	–$2,004	–$2,882	–$7,401	–$5,124
Montana	–$6,267	–$892	–$5,617	–$4,143	–$10,994	–$5,974
Nevada	–$2,754	$599	–$2,104	–$2,652	–$309	$1,997
New Mexico	–$3,368	$1,238	–$2,718	–$2,013	–$6,330	–$6,039
Utah	–$3,193	$525	–$2,543	–$2,727	–$6,029	–$4,963
Wyoming	–$7,219	–$2,836	–$6,569	–$6,088	–$8,442	–$2,891

Source: Bureau of Economic Analysis 1999.

in per capita income from 1978 to 1988, the period that was hardest on the region. In general, the more metropolitan states of Colorado, Arizona, and Nevada and the less metropolitan Idaho saw smaller declines in pay per job than other states did. Colorado and Arizona also saw smaller growth in the gap between state and national per capita income. The least metropolitan states, Montana, New Mexico, and Wyoming, saw the largest declines in real pay. This matches the experience of small and non-metropolitan areas all across the country depicted in figures 2.1 and 2.2.

The numbers in table 2.1 help explain the high level of distress and sense of economic crisis in many parts of the Mountain West. Between 1978 and 1988, per capita income across the country rose by $3,251, more than in any state in the Mountain West. In five of the eight Mountain West states, the increase in per capita income fell short of the national figure by more than $2,600; of these five, two—Montana and Wyoming—actually saw per capita income fall. In 1998, the gap between regional and national pay per job was more than $6,000 in five of the eight states in the region; in Montana it was almost $11,000.

In 1998, the states of the Mountain West found themselves in an ironic and frustrating position. Relative to the rest of the country, both pay per job and per capita income were lower than they had been twenty years before; real pay per job was absolutely lower. But over the same twenty-year period, employment

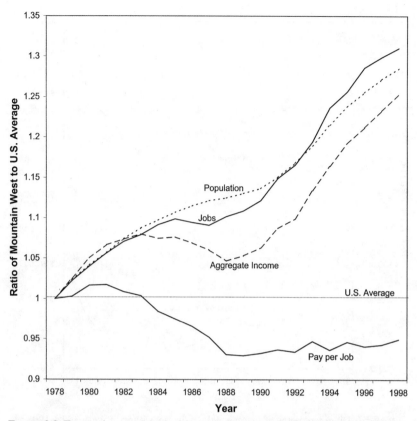

FIGURE 2.3. Economic growth in the Mountain West compared with that in the United States as a whole, 1978–1998. Index of population, jobs, real pay per job, and aggregate real income, Mountain West/United States, 1978 = 1.0. Population, jobs, and aggregate real income rose in relation to the country as a whole; real pay per job fell. *Source:* Bureau of Economic Analysis 1999.

and population had grown more rapidly in the region than in the country as a whole, as had aggregate income during the 1990s.[2] These trends in regional population, employment, aggregate real income, and pay per job relative to the rest of the country are shown in figure 2.3. Clearly, rapid economic expansion could not guarantee rising pay or rapid growth in per capita income.

CONFLICTING TRENDS IN PAY AND INCOME

Because they depict real per capita income rising while pay per job was stagnant or falling, figures 2.1 and 2.2 seem to tell conflicting stories about what was really

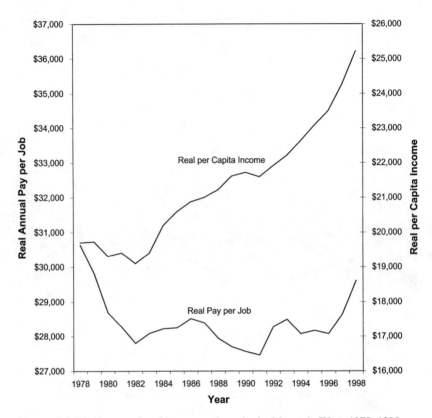

FIGURE 2.4. Divergent paths of income and pay in the Mountain West, 1978–1998. Pay per job fell and partially recovered, whereas per capita income grew steadily after 1982. *Source:* Bureau of Economic Analysis 1999.

happening in the Mountain West during the period 1978–1998. This is illustrated in figure 2.4, in which pay per job and income per capita are plotted in the same space to show just how sharply the two measures diverged. Measured by pay per job, economic well-being declined, with minor interruptions, between 1978 and 1991 and then began a feeble and hesitant recovery. But measured by per capita income, the region did pretty well: after a brief recession-driven dip in the early 1980s, per capita income rose steadily, falling slightly only during the recession year of 1991. Between 1982 and 1998, per capita income rose by one-third; on average, every resident of the region had $6,100 more to spend (in 1998 dollars). How could income rise if jobs were paying less? The answer lies in the different ways in which pay and income are defined and measured.

The word *pay* commonly refers only to labor earnings, that is, the income that workers receive in return for committing their time to particular jobs. But individuals and families receive income from sources other than paychecks. Those who own assets such as savings accounts, bonds, stocks, private pension plans, and real estate receive property income in the form of interest, dividends, rent, and capital gains. And many individuals receive transfer payments from the government: Social Security benefits, unemployment compensation, food stamps, and other income maintenance payments that are not tied to current employment.

These sources of income are not small—about one-third of all income received by Americans comes from non-employment sources—and they have been growing more rapidly than labor earnings. In 1970, non-employment income represented about 23 percent of total income nationally; by 1997, it had risen to 35 percent.

In the Mountain West, non-employment income per person rose by almost 63 percent in real terms between 1978 and 1998. This by itself added $3,000 to per capita income (in 1998 dollars) and was an important factor in explaining how income could rise even when pay growth was sluggish. Figure 2.5 depicts for the Mountain West the trends during the period 1978–1998 in total non-employment income and its components.

Another important factor explaining the divergence between pay and income is that pay per job is calculated by dividing total pay by the number of jobs, whereas income per capita comprises total income from all sources averaged across the whole population, including those who do not work—children, for example, and stay-at-home adults, retirees, and disabled persons. If a larger share of the population holds jobs, income per capita will rise even if pay per job remains unchanged.[3]

Over the last several decades of the twentieth century, the share of the population holding jobs increased, in part because more women sought paid employment.[4] In addition, as post-war baby boomers entered the workforce and birthrates declined, the share of the population of working age increased.[5] As a result of these two developments, the ratio of workers to population increased by 8.3 percent between 1980 and 1998.

Which of these measures—pay per job or per capita income—should we rely on to depict what has happened to living standards in the Mountain West? The question is not just a matter of academic curiosity. How well off we believe residents of the region to be and whether we perceive their circumstances as improving or worsening depends on the measure we select. As it turns out, both measures are useful. Both tell us something important about the well-being of workers and their households. And as measures of well-being, both have weaknesses that are important to understand.

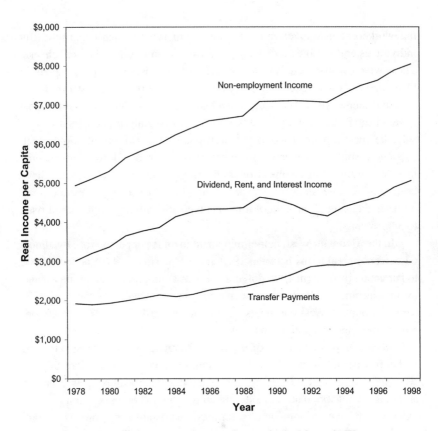

FIGURE 2.5. Real per capita non-employment income in the Mountain West, 1978–1998 (1998 dollars). Both property income (dividend, rent, and interest income) and transfer payments rose in real terms. *Source:* Bureau of Economic Analysis 1999.

RISING INCOME

Rising income contributes to the well-being of households by allowing them to consume more goods and services. In the Mountain West in 1998, higher incomes allowed individuals, on average, to purchase about $6,100 more worth of goods and services (at 1998 prices) than they could have fifteen years earlier, when the economy was beginning its recovery from the 1982 recession; for a family of four the comparable increase was $24,400.[6] But as important as this increased ability to consume may have been—and for most families in the region, $24,400 would have been quite important—it is nevertheless possible to overstate the effect of growing per capita income on the well-being of typical individuals and families.

For one thing, in both the Mountain West and the United States as a whole, income is unequally distributed. This means that a *majority* of individuals have incomes that are below the per capita average and, when the average rises, this majority receives less than the average increase.[7] Thus, only a minority of families saw their incomes increase by $24,000 or more. And the sense that many families were not benefiting from income growth was exacerbated by the fact that after 1978, in both the region and the country as a whole, income inequality increased substantially.

Some of this growth in inequality came from the labor market, in which wage gaps based on education and experience widened. But the growth of non-employment income, which, as we have seen, became relatively more important over the period, also affected some families much more than others. Who got this non-employment income?

Although the percentage of the population over sixty-five years of age did not increase much between 1978 and 1998, the total income of retirees rose dramatically as a result of increased benefits from Social Security, other pension programs, and Medicare reimbursement of health care costs. In fact, nationwide, about two-thirds of transfer payments are retirement-related Social Security and other government pension benefits and Medicare reimbursements; in the Mountain West, these sources account for about 75 percent of transfer payments. At the same time, private savings, including private pension plans, provide interest, dividend, and rental income to retirees. Thus, a large share of the income that does not come from jobs accrues to retired workers and their families. A substantial part of property income, however, flows to investors who are not of retirement age. Because the ownership of property is quite concentrated, property income tends to be relatively more important to high-income families than to less affluent ones.[8] On the other hand, most non-retirement-related transfer payments go to unemployed, disabled, and low-income individuals regardless of their age.

Another reason to suspect that rising incomes and increased well-being may not quite go hand in hand is that, as we have seen, an important source of rising incomes has been an increase in the number of women in the workforce. To the extent that families have succeeded in raising their incomes only by taking more jobs, higher income has come at the cost of reduced time for leisure, household work, or volunteer service in the community.[9] Evidently, families think that receiving additional income outweighs the cost of earning it and that taking more jobs makes them better off—but it is not all gravy.

FALLING PAY PER JOB

Although we recognize that per capita income is an important measure of economic well-being, in the rest of this book we focus primarily on analyzing not the rise in income that occurred in the Mountain West but the fall in pay per job.

As we will explain shortly, what falling pay per job means for workers and their families can be a little ambiguous. Suffice it to say at this point that pay rates are obviously important to people. They indicate how work will be rewarded; influence important decisions families make about where, when, and how much to work; and play a major role in determining family income. In fact, in the economy as a whole, about 65 percent of the incomes people receive come from pay; for some individuals and families, nearly all income is in the form of wages and salaries. For this group, making a distinction between pay and income is not very meaningful.

There are a variety of ways to measure pay—per job, per worker, per hour, per week, and so forth—and each tells us something slightly different. As it turns out, however, only one measure—pay *per job*—really works for our purposes. This is because the central concern of this book is the relationship between the changing industrial structure of the Mountain West—particularly the decline of the region's natural resource industries—and the prosperity of its residents. This relationship rests on what people are paid in different industries, places, and years.[10] And only in the case of pay per job are detailed data available by industry, place, and year.[11]

Pay per Job and Hours of Work

Despite its usefulness in answering questions about industrial structure and earnings, annual pay per job does not always tell us what we want to know about how workers are faring. For one thing, it fails to measure accurately pay per unit of effort, which is conventionally measured by hourly wages. Obviously, the two are related and tend to behave similarly. We can express this relationship for a year-round job in the form of a simple equation:

Pay per job = Pay per hour × Hours per week per job × 50 weeks

Because the weekly hours of work required in different jobs varies, it is quite possible for jobs with the same hourly wage to provide different total pay on an annual basis.[12] And when we observe pay per job falling, we need to understand that this is due in part to falling hourly wages but is also due to an increase in the number of part-time jobs in the labor market and the reduced weekly hours of work those part-time jobs require.

Businesses' payroll data indicate that between 1964 and 1998, the average workweek for jobs across the United States in all industries declined by 4 hours.[13] Over a year, this is equivalent to a reduction of about five or six weeks of work. The average figure, however, masks changes that vary considerably from industry to industry. For manufacturing and construction, the workweek actually increased by about an hour in recent years. For services and retail trade, it declined by 3 and 8 hours, respectively. The decline in average workweek for all jobs is tied to declines within industries such as services and retail trade and to a shift in employment from industries with relatively few part-time jobs (manufacturing, construction, and mining) to industries in which part-time work is much more common (services). Figure 2.6 shows, for the United States as a whole, how the workweek varies from one industry to another and how it has changed in selected industries over time.

Although comparable figures for hours of work are not reported at the state level, it is likely that the same reduction of the workweek observed across the country has also occurred in the Mountain West. Some states do track this statistic; Montana, for example, reports that average weekly hours of work per job have declined faster than the national average.

To the extent that it is driven by falling hourly wages, a fall in pay per job is unambiguously bad. Most people can find satisfying and productive ways other than working for pay to use their time and energy. We call this leisure, but it should be clearly understood that leisure in this sense often involves a lot of hard, albeit unpaid, work: taking care of children, mowing the lawn, volunteering at local schools, and the like. The important point is that leisure is valuable to people, and in deciding to work for pay they face a trade-off between leisure and income. A fall in hourly wages means that the terms of that trade-off have deteriorated and people are worse off.

Consider the case of a single mother whose one job is her only source of income. Imagine that over time, the hourly wages she receives from her employer do not keep up with inflation, even though she continues to work 40 hours per week. Real earnings from her job will fall, and she will obviously be worse off: she will work the same number of hours but have less real income to buy what her family needs. She might be able to maintain her income by taking on another job, but only at the cost of the leisure time she needs to care for her children.

When the decline in pay per job is due to a decline in length of the workweek, however, the significance for workers and their families of falling pay per job is less clear. This is because a reduction in weekly hours of work frees up valuable leisure time, and this can compensate for lower income.

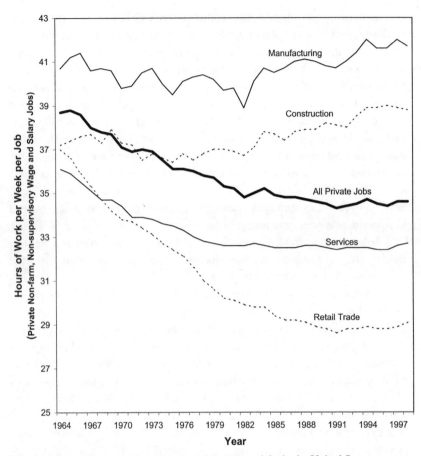

FIGURE 2.6. Trends in weekly hours of work in private jobs in the United States, 1964–1998. Weekly hours rose in manufacturing and construction jobs and fell in services, retail trade, and all private jobs in general. *Source:* Bureau of Labor Statistics 1999b.

Consider now the situation of a woman whose children have reached school age and who thus finds that she finally has time to pursue the career she abandoned a decade or so earlier. She goes back to work part-time because, as attractive as work is for her, she still has responsibilities at home. As a result of her decision to return to work, she must sacrifice some of the leisure time she formerly devoted to working at home, volunteering in the community, or recreation. But she and her family are obviously better off. There is more income to go around, and she is evidently making use of her time in a way she values highly. Obviously, part-time work meets her needs; to the extent that the reduction in earnings per job across the economy is attributable to more workers taking part-time work on this kind of voluntary basis, falling earnings per job signal no loss of well-being.

Finally, consider an example in which an employer responds to market pressures not by reducing hourly wages but by cutting a man's weekly work hours from, say, 42 to 34. Real earnings from his job are down, and unless he can take a second job for 8 hours per week, he will obviously lose some income, which he and his family believe they need. He does have some time now to work around the house and help with the children, and to a degree this makes up for his loss of income. But evidently he would rather have the income; otherwise, he would have opted for part-time work in the first place.

There is ample evidence that workers sometimes prefer more leisure to higher pay and income. Unions have called strikes to reduce the amount of mandatory overtime imposed on workers, a move that would make no sense if pay were all that mattered. Similarly, when during the first half of the twentieth century workers campaigned for a 40-hour workweek, they were making it clear that they preferred additional leisure to higher income.

Workers have different preferences for length of the workweek. Some seek as many hours as possible, especially if they are paid a premium for hours in excess of forty. Others want to limit their time on the job to a "normal" workweek. Still others, with important alternative commitments and interests, will work for pay only if they can find part-time employment. Students, parents with young children, workers with other jobs, retirees, and active community volunteers are all examples of people whose desire to work limited hours can be accommodated by part-time jobs.

If pay per job is falling because workers are choosing to earn less, there is no cause for alarm. But the decision to take part-time work is not always a voluntary one. Some workers would prefer to work more but cannot find a full-time job. To the extent that falling pay per job is due to an involuntary increase in part-time work, it indicates an erosion in the well-being of wage earners.

In its monthly Current Population Survey (CPS), the U.S. Census Bureau asks a large sample of American workers whether they are working less than full-time and if so, why. The responses are grouped into two categories labeled "economic" and "non-economic." Economic reasons for working part-time include inability to find a full-time job even though the worker wants one, slack business conditions, lack of materials, and bad weather. Non-economic reasons include not wanting a full-time job because of child care or other family responsibilities, being retired, being in school, or taking vacation or personal leave days. Because the non-economic reasons involve workers' choosing between taking more hours of work and pursuing other personal and family objectives, these reasons are also labeled "voluntary." Of course, people with young children or sick family members may not experience their part-time status as voluntary. Nevertheless, when they choose to work part-time for "voluntary" reasons, workers are indicating that they have uses for their time that they value more highly than the pay they forgo by not taking a full-time job.[14]

In April 2000, the survey data indicated that 22.6 percent of American workers were working part-time, that is, fewer than 35 hours per week (Bureau of Labor Statistics 2000b). The average workweek for these part-time workers was 24.1 hours. Of these workers, 10.3 percent reported that they worked reduced hours for involuntary reasons; of this group, about one-third reported that they could find only part-time work, even though they wanted to work full-time. Conversely, 89.7 percent of those who worked part-time said that they did so for "non-economic" reasons. For instance, 26 percent had conflicting family obligations, another 27 percent were students, and 10 percent were retired or had health limitations. This survey is conducted monthly and refers to employment status in the week prior to the survey, and 10.5 percent of respondents reported that they were working part-time that week because they had taken personal leave or vacation days (Bureau of Labor Statistics 2000c).

Data on part-time workers in the Mountain West show that reasons for part-time work in the region are similar to those in the United States as a whole; the vast majority of part-time work is reported by workers as voluntary. In both the Mountain West and the country as a whole, the share of part-time work considered involuntary rose during the recession of the early 1980s and declined during the expansion of the 1990s (Bureau of Labor Statistics 1978–1998b).

Since the CPS samples the entire population and reports on work hours for everyone over sixteen years of age, both students and retirees are included in the sample; among these workers, involuntary part-time work was relatively infrequent. For workers aged twenty-five to fifty-four, however, involuntary part-time work was somewhat more common than for the population as a whole; 21 percent of men and 12 percent of women in this age group gave economic reasons for their part-time work. Stated otherwise, even in this case 80 to 90 percent of part-time work was engaged in on a voluntary basis.

The 25 percent of workers who reported working part-time can be contrasted with the 32 percent who reported working more than 40 hours per week, the 20 percent who reported working 49 or more hours per week, and the 9 percent who worked 60 or more hours per week. Clearly, in some sense, part-time workers are "balanced" within the economy by those working more than full-time.

We conclude from this discussion that pay per job can fall because hourly wages go down or there is an involuntary loss of work hours; in both cases, workers are hurt. But some of the decline can be due to voluntary reduction of work hours, from which workers evidently benefit. Pay per job turns out to be an imperfect measure of pay per unit of time or effort (which might best be represented by hourly wages), and the fall in pay per job observed in the Mountain West overstates the degree to which the value of labor in the region has declined.

Pay per Job and Multiple Job Holding

For some purposes, workers and their families may be less interested in how much they can earn per hour or per job than they are in their total yearly earnings; in other words, rather than pay per job, they are interested in annual pay per worker. The two can differ because a worker can hold more than one job. Consider the example of a young, married university student with a small child. He works 30 hours per week in a computer store and, to "make ends meet," tends bar on the weekends. He has two jobs and obviously is not indifferent to what each job pays. But in figuring out how he is going to pay tuition, buy groceries, and heat the house in the winter, what counts is the total earnings generated by both jobs, not the pay associated with each one; that is, what matters here is pay per worker rather than pay per job.

The relationship between pay per job and pay per worker can be represented with an equation:

$$Annual\ pay\ per\ worker = Pay\ per\ job \times Jobs\ per\ worker$$

In non-metropolitan areas, where farmers and ranchers often hold non-agricultural jobs, the difference between pay per worker and pay per job is greater than in urban labor markets, where multiple job holding is less common. Similarly, the increasing incidence of multiple job holding over time means that pay per worker can rise even if pay per job falls. Figure 2.7 shows how these two measures evolved in the Mountain West between 1978 and 1998. As expected, the two measures tended to track each other. But it is also clear that following the recession of 1982, workers began to take on additional jobs, allowing pay per worker to rise while pay per job stagnated. This is reflected in the number of jobs per worker,[15] which between 1984 and 1998 increased in the Mountain West by 12 percent. In the country as a whole, the comparable increase was 7 percent.

This increase in jobs per worker occurred at the same time the number of hours per job was falling, with the result that estimates of average weekly hours per worker (as opposed to weekly hours per job) indicate considerable stability for the country as a whole.[16] When the aging of the population is taken into account, average weekly hours at work in 1993 were almost identical to those in 1976, about 41 (Rones, Ilg, and Gardner 1997), and other evidence shows that the number of weekly hours of market work per worker has been roughly

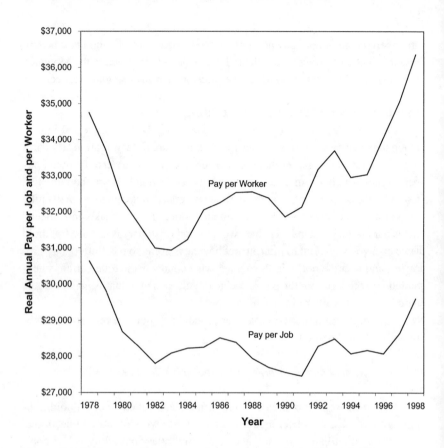

FIGURE 2.7. Real pay per job versus real pay per worker in the Mountain West,
1978–1998 (1998 dollars). Because of increased multiple job holding, pay per worker
could rise while pay per job stagnated. *Source:* Bureau of Economic Analysis 1999.

constant for fifty years (McGrattan and Rogerson 1998). CPS figures for average length of workweek reported by Mountain West workers during 1978–1998
were also quite stable, at about 39 hours per week.[17]

As the number of part-time jobs has grown and pay per job has fallen, workers have been able to maintain or even increase their total earnings by taking on
more jobs. In this sense, the decline in pay per job observed in the Mountain
West overstates the plight of workers and their families. But if they have maintained their earnings only by working more and giving up leisure, they clearly
have been adversely affected.[18] Anecdotally, at any rate, many working families in the Mountain West are behaving in this fashion. They report that in response
to low wages and the increasing prevalence of part-time jobs, they have to work

at several jobs and for longer hours to make ends meet. In this sense, multiple job holding is often seen as a sign that the job market is failing to provide a sufficient number of good, family-wage employment opportunities.

There are, of course, workers who prefer to hold multiple jobs, one or all of which are part-time.[19] Many students at the University of Montana, for example, pursue this strategy, which allows them to earn the income they need and take classes scheduled at odd hours throughout the day. Similarly, many relatively affluent workers take extra jobs because their professional schedules allow it, because their expertise is in demand, and because their financial objectives extend beyond meeting basic living expenses or paying off debts (Amirault 1997). For this group, it is not primarily low earnings that drive multiple job holding.[20]

Fringe Benefits

Pay per job typically fails to include an important element in total labor compensation: the "fringe benefits" many workers receive in the form of employer contributions to health insurance and pension plans, and paid sick, personal, and vacation leave. These non-cash benefits can contribute substantially to workers' total compensation. In 1998, unionized workers received benefit packages that, taken in total, equaled 53 percent of their wage and salary earnings. For all full-time workers, union and non-union, the value of such benefits was 39 percent of wages. For part-time workers, benefits were smaller, only 24 percent of wages.[21]

Given that these non-wage benefit rates vary considerably across different jobs, relative differences in wages from job to job can misstate relative differences in total compensation. But because the value of non-wage benefits is not regularly reported for different industries and geographic areas, we are unable to use figures on total compensation to assess the effect on workers of structural change in the Mountain West. Instead, we must make do with a measure of wages alone.

The use of wages rather than total compensation also potentially disguises a significant negative consequence for workers of moving from a single full-time job to multiple part-time jobs. Although this change in the job mix may leave workers with the same hours of work and the same take-home pay, the difference in fringe benefit rates for full- and part-time work implies that their total compensation is likely to fall.

What Does Falling Pay per Job Mean?

During the last two decades of the twentieth century, pay per job in the Mountain West fell or, at best, stagnated, and these developments are widely viewed as symptoms of an economy in crisis. In chapters 4 and 5, we examine the origins and implications of these trends in pay per job. We chose this measure of pay in part because it is the only one available that is sufficiently comprehensive and detailed to answer our questions. But we recognize that it is incomplete and can be misleading.

For the reasons outlined earlier, we suspect that declining pay per job overstates how badly workers are faring. Some of the decline is attributable to the fact that many workers want to work part-time, whereas others, albeit a relatively small number, take part-time jobs by default rather than choice. At the same time, we know that earnings per worker and income per capita have risen while pay per job declined. In part, this was possible because workers took on additional jobs. For some, taking an extra job was an appealing way of earning extra income; for others, it was an unattractive default strategy that could soften but not eliminate the adverse effects of a deteriorating labor market.

We would like to be able to show how each measure discussed here—income per capita and pay per job, per worker, and per hour—evolved in the Mountain West between 1978 and 1998 and how that evolution differed from one measure to another. Unfortunately, we do not have the hourly wage data to do that.[22] Figure 2.8, however, plots these pay and income measures for Montana and illustrates just how diverse their behavior can be. Even here, however, because there are important differences in the jobs and workers included in each measure, we have to sound a note of caution. In particular, the figures on pay per hour are for non-supervisory wage and salary jobs only; hourly earnings of supervisory employees and self-employed individuals are not counted (Montana Department of Labor and Industry 1999, p. 17). On the other hand, pay per job is calculated for all jobs. Since these two measures refer to different collections of jobs, the relationship between them is not a function of weekly hours of work alone, as described earlier.

RELATIVE PAY AND INCOME OF STATES

Thus far, we have focused on the real pay or income available to support individuals and families. For better or worse, people do not always, or even usually, judge their well-being only on the basis of their personal ability to satisfy their needs and desires. Instead, they often judge how well off they are by comparing themselves with their neighbors. That is, perceived economic well-being is often measured in relative terms. Even if their real income is rising, some people perceive their well-being as deteriorating if their peers' income is rising faster than their own.

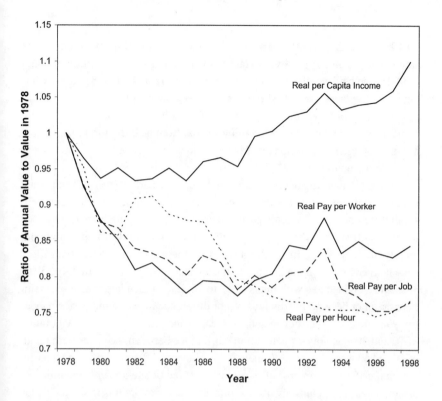

FIGURE 2.8. Trends in different pay and income measures in Montana, 1978–1998. Index of per capita income, pay per worker, pay per job, and pay per hour, in all cases real, 1978 = 1.0. *Source:* Real pay per hour, Montana Department of Labor and Industry 1999; pay per worker, Bureau of Economic Analysis 1999 and Bureau of Labor Statistics 2000a; per capita income and pay per job, Bureau of Economic Analysis 1999.

In the public economic dialogue, this same standard is often applied to the performance of a regional or state economy. The question is not just whether real pay and income are rising, whether employment opportunities are expanding, or whether unemployment is declining. Rather, states and regions compare themselves with one another. If local pay and income are growing, but not as fast as those of other states, the local economy is often seen as lagging or even failing.

One popular way of comparing states is to rank them from best to worst by one measure or another; these ranks and the way they have changed over time are then reported as a measure of economic performance. It is partly on the basis of such measures that the states of the Mountain West have been found wanting, despite rapid growth in employment, population, and total real income.

Table 2.2 displays the per capita income ranks of all the Mountain West states in 1978 and 1998. Every state but Colorado saw its per capita income rank decline between these two years. Wyoming's rank fell by 28 places; Montana's by 15 places. Nevada slid down 9 places, Idaho 7 places, and New Mexico 6 places. For Nevada, the decline in rank was from near the top to not quite so near the top, whereas for Wyoming, it was from near the top to the lowest one-third. Others (Utah and New Mexico) slid from close to the bottom to even closer to the bottom.

Although this way of characterizing the relative performance of economies is popular, it has significant drawbacks. The most important is that relatively small differences in economic performance can lead to quite large differences in rank, particularly when a large number of states are performing at approximately the same level. In 1998, for instance, there was just a 5 percent difference in average per capita income of the ten states with national ranks of 39 to 48 and the eight states with ranks of 19 to 26. Even much larger differences in rank may not be associated with a major difference in economic performance. In 1998, the difference between the per capita incomes of the states with ranks of 10 and 30 was only 14 percent; the difference between the states with ranks of 10 and 40 was 24 percent. Although these income differences may seem large, regional differences in cost of living or the value of site-specific amenities or disamenities could plausibly also be this large (we explore this topic in chapter 5). In any case, the difference between a rank of 10 and a rank of 30 certainly seems larger than 14 percent. It is in this sense that judging relative economic performance by state ranking can be misleading.

Table 2.2. Change in National Ranking of per Capita Incomes of Mountain West States, 1978–1998

State	Rank by Per Capita Income		Change in Rank
	1978	1998	
Arizona	33	35	−2
Colorado	14	6	8
Idaho	36	43	−7
Montana	31	46	−15
Nevada	2	11	−9
New Mexico	42	48	6
Utah	37	40	−3
Wyoming	6	34	−28

Source: Bureau of Economic Analysis 1999.
Note: Highest rank = 1.

Commentators on the performance of the Mountain West's economies often mistakenly move from the correct observation that incomes relative to the national average are declining to the incorrect conclusion that incomes themselves are declining and residents are becoming steadily worse off.

Between 1978 and 1998, per capita income in all the Mountain West states but Colorado grew more slowly than in the country as a whole. As a result, by 1998, the actual increase in real per capita income in these states was less than it would have been had the state grown at the national rate. Table 2.3 shows the actual change in per capita income in Mountain West states from 1978 to 1998, the change that would have been observed if growth rates had matched the national average, and the gap between these two. These gaps are a measure of relative performance; they tell us, in a sense, what might have been. In Wyoming, Montana, and Nevada, they were substantial, ranging between approximately $2,900 and $6,500. In the other states, they were more modest but still significant. As the figures in table 2.3 make clear, there are two ways to assess what was happening in the region. On one hand, for every state but Wyoming, there were substantial gains in per capita income. On the other hand, for every state except Colorado, the gains could be considered deficient by national standards.

For such states as Nevada and Wyoming, which were used to the comfort of above-average incomes, the steep declines to average or below average were also interpreted as evidence of economic failure. But this interpretation of differences in pay and per capita income is correct only if the cost of living and the value of

Table 2.3. Increase in Real per Capita Income in Mountain West States and "Loss" Due to Below-Average Growth, 1978–1998 (1998 Dollars)

State	Actual Increase in per Capita Income, 1978–1998	Increase If per Capita Income Had Grown at National Rate	"Lost" per Capita Income Due to Growth Below National Rate
Arizona	$5,241	$5,925	-$684
Colorado	$8,647	$6,669	$1,977
Idaho	$3,782	$5,716	-$1,935
Montana	$1,927	$6,030	-$4,104
Nevada	$4,750	$7,638	-$2,888
New Mexico	$4,047	$5,348	-$1,301
Utah	$4,638	$5,499	-$862
Wyoming	$852	$7,329	-$6,477

Source: Computed by the authors using data from Bureau of Economic Analysis 1999.

site-specific amenities are similar in the two areas being compared. Because more than 80 percent of the country's population lives in metropolitan areas, with 50 percent living in a small number of very large cities, national per capita income tends to reflect economic and environmental conditions in the country's largest cities. This is not true of per capita incomes in the Mountain West, however, where most residents live in relatively small cities, towns, and rural areas. The Mountain West states of Montana, Idaho, and Wyoming were among the five least metropolitan states in the country; New Mexico was in the bottom one-fourth of the states; Utah was below the national average. As we show in chapter 5, there is good reason to doubt that differences in pay and income across communities of different size reflect comparable differences in real economic well-being.

TIMING OF THE DETERIORATION IN PAY AND INCOME IN THE MOUNTAIN WEST

During the 1980s, all states in the Mountain West saw their relative incomes plummet dramatically; see figures 2.9 and 2.10. For states that had per capita incomes well below the national average to begin with, further declines during the 1980s were doubly disturbing. But it is interesting that the relative deterioration in pay and income in the Mountain West emerged as a significant public policy issue primarily in the second half of the 1990s. This is somewhat surprising since, as all the figures in this chapter show, the absolute and relative declines in various measures of real pay and income took place during the 1980s, with most of the fall occurring in the first half of that decade. The second half of the 1980s was a period of relative stability, and then, during the 1990s, there was modest but ongoing improvement. In this sense, concern about the region's economic decline appears to have come ten to fifteen years too late for the development of a reasoned and effective policy response. With little help from public policy, the issues of the 1980s have begun to resolve themselves.

It is possible that problems associated with lagging state and regional economies in the Mountain West have only recently received attention because the region's residents believed that the rapid growth in the first half of the 1990s would undo the damage done the decade before. When rapid growth in employment, population, and total income did not lead to significant growth in pay and relative incomes, the problem came to be seen as more deeply rooted, tied to structural changes that had taken place in the region over the previous two decades. The relative or absolute decline in the natural resource sectors was one of the more obvious of these structural changes. In this context, the economic problems of the

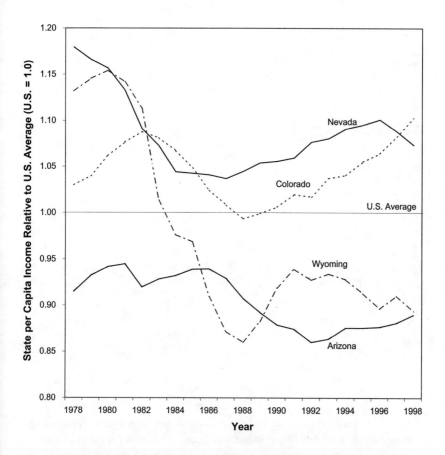

FIGURE 2.9. Per capita incomes in the four higher-income Mountain West states relative to the U.S. average, 1978–1998. In relation to the country as a whole, per capita income changed relatively little in Colorado and Arizona but fell in Nevada and Wyoming. Per capita income in Wyoming started above and ended up below that of the rest of the country. *Source:* Bureau of Economic Analysis 1999.

1980s came to be seen as incurable by general economic growth alone. More attention, it was believed, had to be paid to the structure of economic opportunities that had developed in the region. In the late 1990s, policy makers could look back on a decade of rapid job growth and not like what they saw. Jobs alone had not done the trick, and "good job" promotion became a new imperative.

CONCLUSION

During the early 1980s, real pay *per job* in the Mountain West region declined

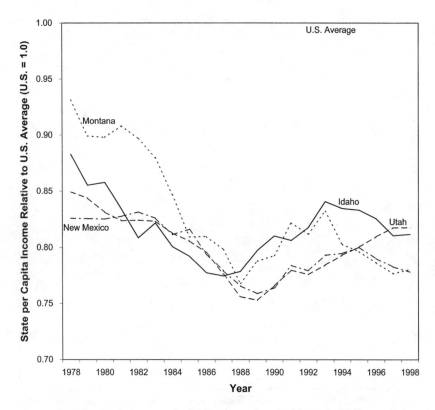

FIGURE 2.10. Per capita incomes in the four lower-income Mountain West states relative to the U.S. average, 1978–1998. All four states started with per capita income below the rest of the country's and experienced some slippage. Relative per capita income in Montana fell the most. *Source:* Bureau of Economic Analysis 1999.

significantly. The Mountain West was not alone in this experience; similar declines occurred in the country's small metropolitan and non-metropolitan areas. *Relative* to the country as a whole, the Mountain West saw even more dramatic declines in both pay per job and per capita income. Despite above-average growth in jobs, population, and aggregate earnings during the 1990s, the Mountain West's absolute and relative losses in the 1980s were not made up.

Figures on pay *per job* are particularly useful as measures of labor market conditions at the county and state levels in a wide variety of industries; this kind of information is needed if we are to assess the role of change in industrial structure in the determination of pay. But as useful as it is, pay per job does not accurately reflect pay *per hour* because of the proliferation of part-time jobs.

Similarly, trends in pay per job and pay per worker have diverged as workers have taken on multiple jobs. This multiple job holding has allowed pay per worker to rise steadily since the mid-1980s.

Real per capita incomes also rose steadily in the Mountain West through-out the second half of the 1980s and the 1990s. Per capita incomes were able to rise despite falling or stagnant pay per job because of multiple job holding, an increase in the percentage of the population holding jobs, and the rising impor-tance of non-employment income. Non-employment income rose because of increased flows of dividend, interest, and rental income and because of the increas-ing importance of private and government retirement programs such as Social Security and Medicare.

The implications for economic well-being of the decline in average weekly hours per job, the rise in multiple job holding, and the increased percentage of the population holding jobs are not entirely clear. Critics often find themselves holding inconsistent positions, both decrying the rise in part-time employment because it reduces earnings potential and criticizing the increase in multiple job holding because it involves too much time at work. From an economic perspec-tive, these trends should be judged against workers' preferences rather than some predefined optimal workweek. In addition, time spent away from paid employ-ment should not be looked upon as merely underemployment. People make many different valuable uses of their time, including raising families, engaging in home-based work, pursuing training and education, and enjoying a variety of service, recreation, and hobby activities. At the same time, paid employment is an impor-tant source of satisfaction and identity quite apart from the monetary rewards. This makes the motivation for labor market decisions quite complex. There is not just one appropriate pattern of time commitments between paid work and other activities. Labor markets work well when they provide a mix of employment opportunities that matches both workers' and firms' preferences.

The decline in per capita income in the Mountain West relative to that in the rest of the country can be interpreted as reflecting a growing gap in eco-nomic well-being only if there are no site-specific differences in the cost of liv-ing and the value of amenities between the region and the country at large. But because most of the region's residents live in small cities and towns and most other Americans live in large metropolitan areas, it seems unlikely that such an assumption is warranted. This issue is explored in chapter 5.

NOTES

1. There is an extensive economic literature on the pitfalls of interpreting per capita

income in this way; for a brief review, see Goodstein 1999. Many of these critiques focus on the fact that a variety of public goods (e.g., schools) and "bads" (e.g., air pollution) affect our well-being, but income has little to do with how much of them we experience.

2. Aggregate (or total) real income is the sum of all income for all families and individuals in a region or in the country as a whole. Between 1983 and 1989, aggregate income growth was slightly lower in the Mountain West region than in the rest of the country.

3. Consider a family of four with $10,000 in non-wage income. If one member of the family holds a $30,000-per-year job, total family income is $40,000 and income per capita is $10,000. If two members hold $30,000-per-year jobs, total family income is $70,000 and income per capita is $17,500.

4. The ratio of the female labor force to the female population rose by 19.7 percent between 1980 and 1998, from .477 to .571. For males, the ratio fell very slightly (by 0.6 percent) over the same period, from .720 to .716 (U.S. Census Bureau 1999b, table 651).

5. Nationally, the percentage of the population aged twenty-five to fifty-four rose from 37.8 to 43.6 percent between 1980 and 1998 (U.S. Census Bureau 1999b, table 14).

6. Some of the increased income of families, of course, was used to pay taxes and therefore provided public goods and services from which families indirectly benefited.

7. A majority of individuals can have below-average incomes because the distribution of income is skewed, which means there are a small number of individuals with very high incomes. Consider a group of five people, four of whom have incomes of $25,000 and one of whom has an income of $75,000. The total income of the group is $175,000, and per capita (or average) income is $35,000. Thus, a majority (80 percent in this example) of individuals in the group have incomes below the average.

8. For example, in 1996, average adjusted gross income (AGI) on federal individual income tax returns was about $50,000. On the 71 percent of returns reporting AGI of less than $50,000, 5.7 percent of AGI was from dividends, interest, capital gains, and rents and royalties. This percentage rose to 14.2 for all returns reporting AGI in excess of $50,000 and to 22.3 for those reporting AGI of more than $100,000. Calculated from Internal Revenue Service data as reported in U.S. Census Bureau 1999b, table 561.

9. This comment should not be taken as a criticism either of women who decide to enter the workforce or of efforts to reduce sex discrimination and expand opportunities for women in the labor market.

10. Changes in industrial structure at the regional level are unlikely to affect non-employment sources of income for the region's residents. This is because the assets that generate people's property income (dividends, interest payments, rents, and so forth) are generally located across the national (or even global) economy and not confined to the region alone. Similarly, the policies that govern the flow of transfer payment income, particularly those of the federal government, are unlikely to be affected by

changes in regional economic structure.

11. Using data from the Regional Economic Information System (Bureau of Economic Analysis 1999), we can calculate earnings per job for every year for a large, detailed list of industries and for geographic areas as broad as the whole country and as narrow as particular counties and urban areas. No other measure of pay is available on this basis. See the appendix for a fuller discussion of how the number of jobs and workers is measured.

12. Since we are measuring pay per full-year equivalent job and assume that such a job involves fifty weeks of work per year, the only way to raise or lower annual hours of work is to raise or lower weekly hours. In fact, a full-year equivalent job may involve slightly more or fewer than fifty weeks of work per year, but we believe this source of variation in annual hours is negligible. For more on this point, see the appendix.

13. National data on hours of work in general and for specific industries are from Bureau of Labor Statistics 1999a. These figures apply to only a portion of all jobs in the economy. See the preceding note.

14. One demographic group that has "voluntarily" reduced its work hours sharply is young, poorly educated males. It seems likely that one reason why these men have decided to work less is that they face extremely limited and dispiriting formal employment opportunities and, in some cases, can find much better-paying work in the illegal economy. This is obviously nothing to be satisfied with; we explore its implications further in chapter 7.

15. To measure the behavior of jobs per worker over time, we use the ratio of jobs, as reported by the Regional Economic Information System, to labor force, as reported by the Bureau of Labor Statistics (2000a). The former data are developed from surveys of establishments; the latter, from the CPS. Given the differences in data sources, the number of jobs per worker we compute implies a larger incidence of multiple job holding than that reported in the CPS by workers themselves (Bureau of Labor Statistics 1999b). For that reason, we use our figure to represent *trends* in multiple job holding but not to compare levels across geographic areas.

16. There is some controversy over how many hours workers actually put in at their jobs. Some analysts see a rise in the number of hours and speak in terms of the "overworked American" (Schor 1991), whereas others insist that the workweek has been overestimated (Robinson and Godbey 1997, chap. 5).

17. If anything, workers in the Mountain West were working slightly longer (by 1 hour) workweeks in the early 1990s than they were in the early 1980s (Bureau of Labor Statistics 1978–1998a).

18. In economic theory, increasing work hours in response to declining wages in known as the "backward-bending supply of labor." Working more when the rewards for working are falling may appear anomalous, but it is a perfectly rational response for people who would rather sacrifice leisure than income. See Filer, Hamermesh, and Rees 1996, pp. 54–60, for an exposition of the theory of choice in hours of work.

19. It is important to emphasize that workers who work fewer than 35 hours per week and those who work more than 35 hours per week in multiple part-time jobs are not the same people. As we saw earlier, workers in the former group reported to the CPS that in most cases they work part-time voluntarily. But this tells us nothing about the preferences of the latter group, specifically whether they like to hold several part-time jobs or would prefer a single full-time one instead.

20. Data from the CPS indicate that multiple job holding is as common among high-income individuals as it is in the workforce at large.

21. Fringe benefit rates were calculated by the authors as (Hourly total compensation – Hourly wages and salaries) / Hourly wages and salaries, as reported in U.S. Census Bureau 1999b, table 707. Figures refer to private employment only.

22. Data on average hourly pay and average workweek per job are quite limited. For many jobs, firms base pay not on hourly wages but on weekly or monthly salary; in these cases, hourly pay and hours of work cannot be determined from the firms' payroll records. As a result, such pay and hour information is available only for certain types of jobs. In manufacturing, hourly data are available only for production workers, and in service jobs, data are available only for private non-supervisory workers. Thus, a substantial part of the workforce is not covered by the available hourly data. Moreover, because the Bureau of Labor Statistics gathers data from a sample of business firms, the agency is not confident of the data's accuracy at other than the national level. As a result, consistent data on average hourly wages and average workweek per job are not available at the state level.

CHAPTER 3

The Changing Structure of the Mountain West Economies

European settlement of the western frontier forms an important part of American folklore. Spanish soldiers, adventurers, and priests established agricultural settlements in the Southwest centuries before Europeans entered the northern Rocky Mountains. Hard on the heels of the Lewis and Clark Expedition (1804–1806), mountain men spread across the northern part of the Mountain West in pursuit of the valuable furs available for harvest. They and the trading companies they represented established the first commercial outposts in the region. Decades later, livestock operations as far south as Texas began driving cattle to the grasslands that hugged the mountains to the north and west, as far away as Montana and Wyoming. The discovery of precious metals led to a series of gold rushes that constantly shifted from place to place as strikes were made and exhausted. Densely populated mining towns sprang into existence in a matter of months and then, within a few years, disappeared. Montana's territorial capital, for instance, shifted from one such mining town to another as people moved on in pursuit of the next gold field.

The mines and railroads as well as the general population required timber, and local lumber mills were developed to serve that need. As gold operations played out, silver and then copper became the object of more sustained mining and smelting operations. The independent miner gave way to large national corporations that employed thousands of workers in the mines, smelters, and lumber mills. These urban workers struggled with the mine and mill owners over pay and working conditions; by the middle of the twentieth century, they were represented by powerful unions and were earning wages well above what other workers in the region could hope to receive. In the late 1970s, mining and metal-processing workers in the Mountain West earned about $56,000 per year in today's dollars, almost twice the average annual pay in the region, and timber industry workers earned about one-third more than the average.

The last half of the nineteenth century and the first part of the twentieth century also brought homesteaders who settled in the Great Plains portions of Montana, Wyoming, and Colorado to raise crops rather than graze cattle. Moving farther west, farmers broke sod and planted crops in mountain valleys and river basins throughout the region. The first major public irrigation projects were constructed to facilitate this crop-based settlement.[1]

All these settlers—the cowboy and rancher, the prospector and hard rock miner, the lumberjack and homesteader—became enduring symbols of the Old West. In a region defined by its dramatic landscapes, they depended on the land for their livelihood, and entire communities and local economies depended on their success. With a very dispersed population and limited markets, money appeared to flow into the region only as a result of the export of natural resources. Very little manufacturing took place that was not related to those natural resources, and without ranchers, miners, and loggers to sell to, railroaders, storekeepers, whiskey drummers, and blacksmiths would have failed as well.

However convincing this portrait of the regional economy may have been in the past and however important it was in defining the region's identity, it is today largely anachronistic. In just a few decades, the structure of the economy has changed markedly and a "New West" has emerged. Central to this process of change have been the diminishing fortunes of natural resource industries.

DECLINE IN THE NATURAL RESOURCE INDUSTRIES

Like it or not—and there are plenty of strong opinions of either side of the issue—residents of the region now generally acknowledge that they live in the New West, where population and economic activity seem to grow at dizzying speed and people earn their living in very different ways from the way they did in the past. The industrial structure of the region—the mix of goods and services produced and the distribution of employment among these different lines of production—has changed remarkably, and as already noted, many of the region's residents believe it has changed for the worse. Structural change, they argue, has meant that good jobs have disappeared only to be replaced by bad ones, undermining the ability of workers and their families to earn a decent living.

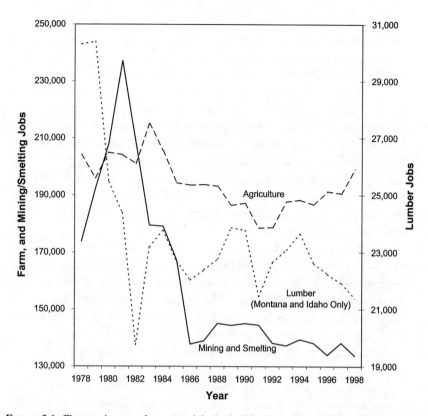

FIGURE 3.1. Changes in natural resource jobs in the Mountain West, 1978–1998. The number of jobs declined sharply in mining and smelting across the region and in lumber and wood products in Montana and Idaho. The increase in agricultural jobs after 1991 is attributable to a change in data reporting (see the text). *Source:* Bureau of Economic Analysis 1999.

The change in industrial structure of particular concern has been the decline in relative importance of the natural resource industries.

Figure 3.1 depicts the tens of thousands of jobs that were lost in natural resource industries in the Mountain West between 1979 and 1998. In metal mining and smelting alone, 103,000 jobs, almost 44 percent of total employment in the industry, were lost between 1981 and 1998. The 1980s were also harsh in farming and ranching. Droughts and weak markets forced ongoing consolidation of farms and ranches into larger but fewer operations. Total agricultural employment in the region declined steadily from the mid-1980s to the early 1990s, with more than 36,000 jobs lost. After 1992, the number of agricultural jobs began to rise steadily, but this increase appears to have been due to the part-time and "hobby" farms and ranches that proliferated during the 1990s with the growth of rural populations and the subdivision of large agricultural holdings.[2]

The history of the lumber and wood products industry in the Mountain West is somewhat more complex. During the early 1980s, employment in this industry plunged by 35 percent as a prolonged national depression in home building led to layoffs and mill closures throughout the region. While shut down, these mills adopted new laborsaving technologies such that when they reopened they required a significantly smaller workforce. In the northern states of Montana and Idaho, where the lumber industry is concentrated, the loss of jobs was significant and permanent. In 1978, these two states accounted for 60 percent of the region's wood products employment, and by 1998 they had seen 9,000 jobs in the industry disappear, a decline of 30 percent.

During the 1990s, however, the ongoing expansion of the national economy boosted home building, and the resulting growth in demand for lumber, along with greater constraints on the regional timber supply, increased wood product prices. These higher prices justified more labor-intensive harvest and processing methods. Outside of Montana and Idaho, the net result was that by 1994, overall lumber and wood products employment had returned to levels similar to those of the late 1970s, and by 1998 it was 11 percent higher. Although production of lumber products throughout the region was relatively stable, the shift of production away from Montana and Idaho caused more economic disruption in the timber-dependent communities of those states than this stability would suggest. Table 3.1 shows the dates and magnitudes of the large declines these industries experienced.

We could argue that the decline in natural resource employment during the 1980s was simply a retreat from a peak established in the late 1970s to levels more typical of the preceding decade. As depicted in figure 3.2, by the mid-1980s total regional employment in mining, metal processing, lumber, and agriculture had stabilized at a level similar to that of fifteen years before.

Table 3.1. Periods of Acute Job Loss in Natural Resource Industries in the Mountain West

Industry	Time Period	Jobs Lost	Percentage Job Loss
Agriculture	1983–1992	36,400	17%
Mining and smelting	1981–1998	103,500	44%
Lumber and wood products	1978–1991	13,500	26%

Source: Bureau of Economic Analysis 1999.

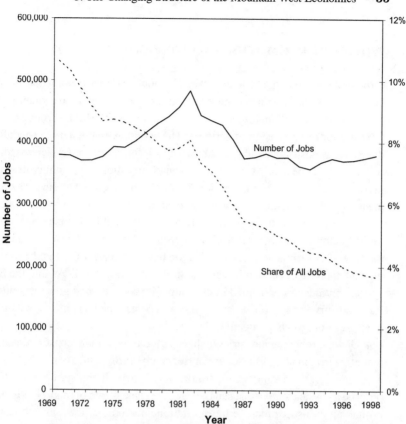

FIGURE 3.2. Natural resource industries' declining share of all jobs in the Mountain West, 1969–1998. The number of jobs in natural resource industries hit a peak in the early 1980s and then began to decline, but as a share of all jobs, natural resource jobs declined steadily over the period. *Source:* Bureau of Economic Analysis 1999.

But it would be misleading to say that aside from short-term booms and busts, natural resource employment has been stable since the 1970s. Certainly such a statement would be of little comfort to laid-off workers and disrupted communities. Moreover, in regard to changes in the region's economic structure, it is the *share* of natural resource industries in total employment that tells the most dramatic story. Even though the number of natural resource jobs has changed little since the 1970s, the natural resource share of total employment has declined by two-thirds, with the result that natural resource industries now directly provide only one of every thirty jobs in the Mountain West. However large the natural resource industries may still loom in the American imagination as symbols of the Old West, in the economy of the New West their economic stature has been sharply diminished.

THE SHIFT FROM GOODS TO SERVICES

Structural change in the Mountain West did not occur in a vacuum. During the last quarter of the twentieth century, the structure of the national economy was rapidly evolving as employment and economic activity shifted from production of goods to provision of services. The economy that emerged was often described as post-industrial or as knowledge, information, or service based. In order to describe exactly what this change in national economic structure involved, what the "shift to services" was all about and what these changes meant to the Mountain West, we need to clarify what we mean by services.

All economic activity is conventionally classified by industry according to the Standard Industrial Classification (SIC) system, which is maintained by the federal government; this classification has been widely used in the reporting and analysis of economic statistics at the industrial level.[3] Within the SIC system, an industry is defined by the output it produces, and given its output, each industry in the SIC classification can be described as either goods-producing or non-goods-producing.

Goods-producing industries include agriculture, mining, construction, and manufacturing; each of these, of course, can be further subdivided.[4] As their name implies, the distinguishing feature of industries in this group is that they produce a physical output that can be stored for some period of time. Non-goods-producing industries include transportation and communications; wholesale and retail trade; finance, insurance, and real estate; services; and government; and again, the broad categories can be subdivided. They are distinguished by the fact that they must produce their outputs, which cannot be stored, on demand.[5]

In the SIC system and in most research and analysis of industrial-level data, only particular kinds of non-goods-producing activities are considered services. These include business and repair services, personal services, entertainment and recreational services, and professional services. Examples include the work of physicians, accountants, advertising copywriters, automobile mechanics, hotel housekeepers, and personal athletic trainers. In popular usage, however, the term *services* is sometimes used more expansively to include all non-goods-producing industries.[6] To avoid any confusion on this point, when we refer to services in this book we mean just those non-goods-producing industries that are considered services in the SIC system; when we refer to non-goods-producing industries, we mean the larger set of industries including services.

About 80 percent of all jobs in the economy of the Mountain West are in non-goods-producing industries, and 30 percent are in services. Similarly, about 50 percent of total personal income comes from earnings in non–goods production, and only 20 percent comes from earnings in services. A more important dif-

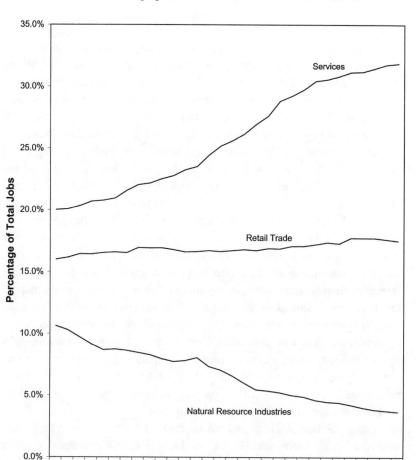

FIGURE 3.3. Changes in the sources of jobs in the Mountain West, 1969–1998. The share of all jobs generated by natural resource industries declined steadily while the retail trade share remained almost constant and the services share grew substantially. *Source:* Bureau of Economic Analysis 1999.

ference between these two categories is that although there has been a substantial shift in employment away from goods production and toward non–goods production, the shift specifically to services has been even more pronounced. Many non-goods-producing activities tend to expand at about the same pace as the economy at large, but that is not true of services; their share of total employment has been steadily increasing.

Figure 3.3 traces trends in the shares of jobs in services, retail trade, and the natural resource industries from 1969 to 1998 in the Mountain West. It is particularly important to note that the shift toward services was not accompanied by a shift toward employment in retail trade; retail trade's share of total employment in the region remained about 17 percent during that period. On the other hand, the share of jobs in services increased by almost two-thirds, from 20 to 33 percent.

The stability of the share of retail trade in total employment is important because it is among the most poorly paid sectors in the economy. This means that if employment opportunities had shifted primarily toward trade, there might well have been significant deterioration in the quality of jobs. Indeed, many residents of the Mountain West believe that this is what happened. As national retailers and fast-food franchises mushroomed across the region, it seemed obvious that everybody must have been working at the minimum wage as salesclerks, grocery baggers, or burger flippers. But again, the shift to services, which did happen, did not mean growth in the share of employment in retail trade.[7]

The workforce in service industries, in which the disproportionate growth in employment is taking place, is quite heterogeneous. These workers include highly paid professionals such as physicians, software writers, lawyers, accountants, and engineers. But they also include some of the lowest-paid workers in the labor force: day care attendants, hotel maids, and domestic workers. As a result, there is no single way to characterize the quality of jobs in service industries. They certainly cannot be categorically dismissed as inferior to goods-producing jobs, especially since a growing number of the latter are held by unskilled workers and paid at the minimum wage.

Figure 3.4 illustrates just how dramatic the shift to services was in the Mountain West between 1969 and 1998. Over this period, service industries added 2.6 million jobs, almost a fivefold increase. In all non-goods-producing industries, employment increased by 6 million jobs, a threefold increase. During the same time, employment in goods production increased by only approximately 1 million jobs, about a twofold increase. Goods production was left behind as the economy of the Mountain West restructured itself; 86 percent of all new jobs were in non–goods production.

The shift away from goods production is even more impressive if we step back to the most recent period of peak goods production, the time of World War II. In 1942, 50 percent of all earnings in the Mountain West were from goods production.[8] But between 1942 and 1996, the share of earnings derived from goods was cut in half while the share derived from non–goods production increased by 50 percent (Bureau of Economic Analysis 2000). From positions of equality in 1942, the paths of goods-producing and non-goods-producing industries diverged so sharply that by century's end, non–goods production was almost three times as important as goods production as a source of earnings. This is illustrated in figure 3.5.

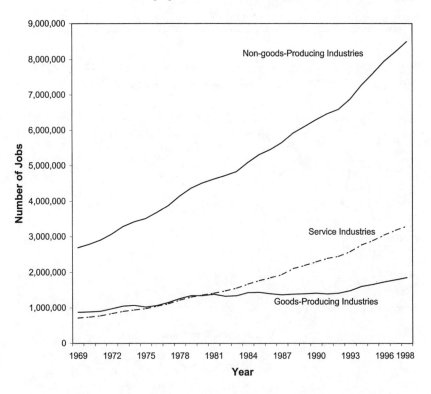

FIGURE 3.4. Growth of goods-producing and non-goods-producing jobs in the Mountain West, 1969–1998. Jobs in non–goods production, particularly services, grew faster than jobs in goods production. *Source:* Bureau of Economic Analysis 1999.

The Declining Role of Labor Earnings in Total Personal Income

In chapter 2, we noted that non-employment income has been an important factor contributing to the growth of per capita income in the Mountain West since the mid-1980s. This income, which consists of returns from investments, rentals from property, and a variety of transfer payments, grew more rapidly than labor earnings from any source until the 1990s, when its share of total income stabilized. See figure 3.6.

CHANGES IN THE RURAL MOUNTAIN WEST

The residents of the Mountain West states are not primarily rural. Almost three-fourths of the region's population lives in metropolitan areas—cities and their

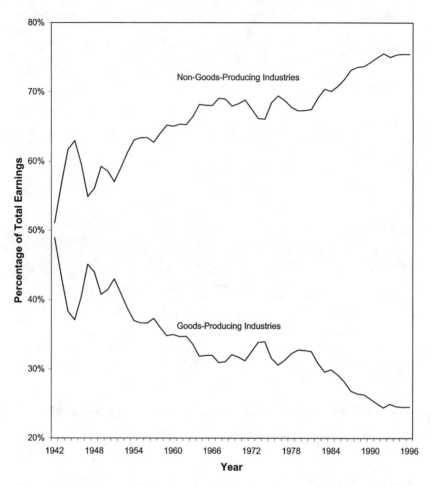

FIGURE 3.5. Long-term shift from goods-producing to non-goods-producing activities in the Mountain West, 1942–1996. The share of earnings from goods production declined steadily during the period. Source: U.S. Census Bureau 1999a.

suburbs—of 50,000 or more. In contrast, residents of comparable metropolitan areas make up 80 percent of the U.S. population as a whole. In 1998, the metropolitan areas of Denver and Phoenix each had about 2.5 million residents, Salt Lake City and Las Vegas each had 1.3 million, Albuquerque and Tucson each approached 750,000, and there were sixteen smaller cities with populations of 60,000 to 400,000.

Although most residents of the Mountain West no longer make their homes on the range, the pattern of urban and rural living varies from state to state. The urbanization rate—the percentage of the population living in metropolitan areas—

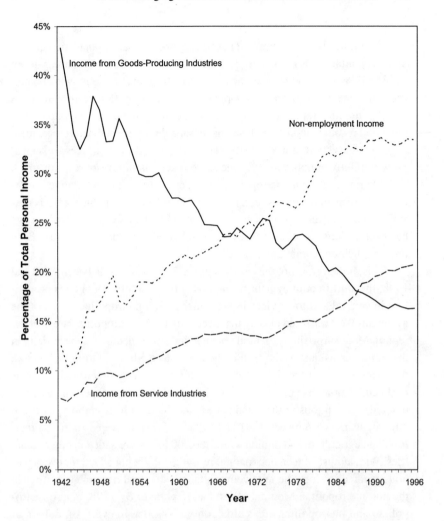

FIGURE 3.6. Changes in the sources of income—goods production, services, and non-employment income—in the Mountain West, 1942–1996. At the beginning of the period, goods production was the major source of personal income in the region; by the late 1980s, both services and non-employment income accounted for a larger share than goods production. *Source:* U.S. Census Bureau 1999a.

is higher in Nevada, Arizona, and Colorado than in the country as a whole. Compared with the country as a whole, the rate is slightly lower in Utah and much lower in Wyoming, Montana, Idaho, and New Mexico.[9] Across the region, this urbanization rate ranges from almost 90 percent in Nevada to about 33 percent in Wyoming, Montana, and Idaho.

Over time, the Mountain West has become more urban as population growth in metropolitan areas has outstripped that in small towns and rural areas. From 1978 to 1998, the population of the region's metropolitan areas grew by 66 percent while the non-metropolitan population increased by 35 percent.[10] It seems possible that this rapid urban growth could explain the declining importance of natural resource industries. It seems reasonable to expect that as cities grow, the economic activities in which they specialize—trade and services—also will grow in relative importance. By the same token, natural resource industries, which rarely operate in metropolitan areas, ought to decline in relative importance. If urbanization drives region-wide structural change in this way, it is possible that outside the metropolitan areas of the Mountain West, structural change has been minimal and natural resource and goods-producing activities have retained their economic dominance.

This, however, is not the case. As figure 3.7 illustrates, between 1969 and 1998, the shift in employment from goods production to non–goods production in general and to services in particular in non-metropolitan areas of the Mountain West mirrored closely that occurring in the metropolitan areas of the region. More surprisingly, natural resource industries declined substantially in these rural areas, just as they did in the region as a whole. During this period, the share of jobs in farming, ranching, and mining in non-metropolitan areas declined by more than one-half, from 20 percent to less than 9 percent, as a dramatic decline in jobs in these industries coincided with strong job growth in other industries.[11] Between 1981 and 1998, 50,000 jobs were lost in non-metropolitan agriculture and mining while 800,000 jobs were added in other industries. With almost sixteen non–natural resource jobs being added for every natural resource job lost, the relative importance of natural resource industries in the non-metropolitan Mountain West had to plunge. By 1998, in non-metropolitan and metropolitan areas alike, only about one in every six dollars of income originated in goods production.

The share of jobs provided by services increased by about 60 percent all across the region between 1969 and 1998, in both metropolitan and non-metropolitan areas, while non–goods production in general expanded somewhat more rapidly in small towns and rural areas than elsewhere. In non-metropolitan areas, 92 percent of all new jobs created between 1978 and 1998 were in non-goods-producing industries.

Although they have changed in similar ways, the industrial structures of metropolitan and non-metropolitan areas still differ. Metropolitan areas remain trade and service centers: in metropolitan areas, services are the source of 34 percent of all jobs, as opposed to 26 percent in non-metropolitan areas. As a

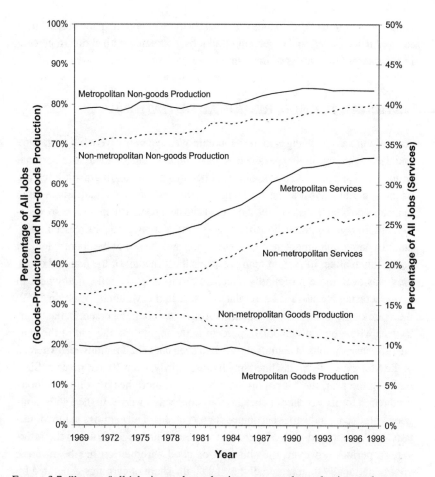

FIGURE 3.7. Shares of all jobs in goods production, non–goods production, and services in metropolitan and non-metropolitan areas of the Mountain West, 1969–1998. In metropolitan areas, non–goods production and services accounted for a larger share of all jobs, and goods production accounted for a smaller share, than in non-metropolitan areas. *Source:* Bureau of Economic Analysis 1999.

result, goods production remains significantly more important in the latter, where in 1998 it accounted for 20 percent of all jobs, compared with about 16 percent in the metropolitan areas of the region.

NATIONAL TRENDS, REGIONAL DEVIATIONS

As profound as the changes in the Mountain West economy were between 1969 and 1998, the region's experience was not unique; across the entire national economy, a similar transformation was occurring. The distinguishing feature of the Mountain West's restructuring was the decline of the natural resource industries on which, historically, the region had depended. But in other respects— the shift from goods production to non–goods production and the increased importance of non-employment income—the region and the rest of the country looked pretty much alike. In fact, in many respects the structure of the national economy was even more profoundly altered. For instance, overall employment in manufacturing has always been relatively low in the Mountain West; in 1969, the share of the labor force in manufacturing was about 25 percent in the country as a whole but only about 10 percent in the region. By the end of the century, the share of jobs in manufacturing had been cut in half nationwide, whereas in the Mountain West it declined much more slowly, from 10 to 8 percent. Similarly, in the past, the Mountain West has relied more heavily on non–goods production for its paychecks than has the country as a whole. In the 1960s, non-goods-producing industries accounted for 65 percent of all earnings in the Mountain West, compared with 57 percent for the country as a whole. In the intervening period, however, the shift out of goods production has been much greater nationally than regionally; by 1998, the share of earnings generated by non-goods-producing industries—78 percent in the region and 76 percent in the United States as a whole—was almost the same.

In some respects, the experiences of the region and the country were identical. For example, changes in the share of non-employment income in total income tracked each other closely. Figure 3.8 illustrates some of these differences and similarities in the national and regional patterns of structural change.

An interesting implication of these diverse patterns of structural change is that from the 1970s through the end of the twentieth century the Mountain West became more like the rest of the country, but not because it went through particularly wrenching changes that more sharply reduced the importance of its goods-producing industries. Rather, the country's industrial structure became more like that of the Mountain West. The region, being less committed to the

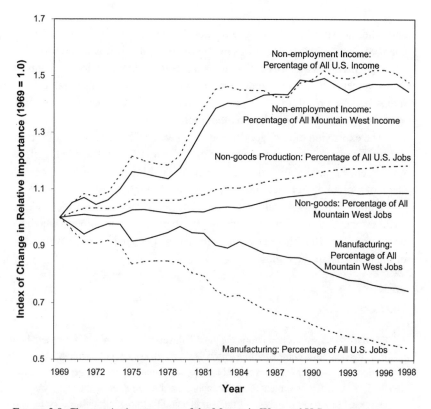

FIGURE 3.8. Changes in the structure of the Mountain West and U.S. economies, 1969–1998. Manufacturing employment fell more rapidly and non-goods-producing employment rose more rapidly in the United States as a whole than in the region. As a result, the structures of the national and regional economies began to resemble each other more closely. *Source:* Bureau of Economic Analysis 1999.

industrial processes that dominated the national economy during the first half of the century, was less vulnerable to the declines in manufacturing that swept the country as the century drew to a close.

CONCLUSION

Over the last three decades of the twentieth century, the structures of both the Mountain West economy and the national economy were dramatically transformed. The most fundamental aspects of this transformation were a decline in relative importance of goods production and a rise in services, trade, finance, and other non-goods-producing activities. In the country as a whole, this sea change in economic structure was more sweeping than it was in the Mountain West and involved a sharp decline in manufacturing. In the region, by contrast, the movement out of goods production centered on the decline of natural resource industries. As a result of these processes, the regional and national economic structures came to resemble each other more closely.

The expansion of non–goods production was led by the growth of service industries, which generated an increasing share of all jobs. Despite the growing presence of national corporate retailers in the Mountain West, the region's share of employment in retail trade remained relatively constant.

Although it was not alone in doing so, the Mountain West did undergo changes in its industrial structure during this period. The question to which we now turn is the effect these structural changes had on the economic well-being of the residents of the region.

NOTES

1. Of course, indigenous populations in the Southwest engaged in agriculture and built irrigation systems centuries before Europeans arrived on the scene. Similarly, Hispanic settlers in the Southwest developed communal irrigation systems centuries before the U.S. federal government began financing irrigation projects in the early twentieth century. For a recent analysis of the Anasazi and Puebloan agricultural systems of the Southwest prior to Spanish settlement, see Stuart 2000.

2. The Census of Agriculture shows that between 1992 and 1997, although the number of farm and ranch operators in the Mountain West reporting agriculture as their principal job fell by 4 percent, the number reporting that agriculture was *not* their primary job rose by 13 percent (U.S. Department of Agriculture 1998a). In addition, the U.S. Department of Labor projects that the occupation in which the most jobs will be lost between 1998 and 2008 is that of farm or ranch manager (Kelinson and Tate 2000, p. 9). Relatively minor or casual agricultural activities can appear in the data as "jobs." Any individual who reports gross farm revenues of $1,000 or more is considered a farm operator in the Census of Agriculture. This would include, for example, a person who sells a single horse for $1,000 or more.

3. All industry-level data cited in this book are classified according to the SIC system. The federal government has adopted the new North American Industry Classification System (NAICS) and will report on that basis in the future. For an overview of NAICS, see National Technical Information Center 1997. A detailed description of the SIC system is provided in Office of Management and Budget 1987.

4. In the SIC system, firms are grouped into industries at several levels of detail. At the broadest level, firms are placed in ten major divisions lettered A through J, of

which agriculture, mining, construction, manufacturing, and retail trade are examples. These divisions can be broken into a set of major groups, each identified with a two-digit number. Thus, "food and kindred products," with SIC code 20, is a major group within manufacturing (division D). Each group is further subdivided into a more detailed list of industries identified with a three-digit number; for example, the "dairy products" industry (SIC code 202) is a component of "food and kindred products." Further division of three-digit industries into yet more detailed components is also provided for, although in this study we employ no data at that level of disaggregation. Some confusion arises because in different contexts, groupings at any of these levels of detail can be considered "industries"; for example, it is appropriate to describe both agriculture (a major division) and dairy products (a three-digit industry) as industries. Moreover, it is sometimes appropriate to create a grouping of industries that crosses major division lines. We do that here by including in natural resource industries not only agriculture and mining (major divisions) but also "lumber and wood products" and "primary metal industries," both of which are two-digit groups within manufacturing.

5. The distinction between outputs that are goods and those that are not goods can seem a little arbitrary at times. Fresh milk, which is a product of agriculture, is considered a good, whereas a freshly cooked meal, which is a product of retail trade, is not.

6. For example, many people might say that banking is a service industry. In some senses, of course, it is; but in the SIC system, banking is considered part of the finance, insurance, and real estate industry rather than the service industry.

7. It may seem surprising that retail trade did not grow in relative importance in the Mountain West, given the increasing and very visible presence of large corporate retailers in the region. Obviously, these firms added jobs. But they also displaced jobs in locally owned retail establishments. Consumers in small towns shifted their purchases to regional trade centers, and in many cities downtown business districts languished.

8. The demand for war matériel no doubt inflated goods production, but the effect appears to have been small. In 1929, goods-producing industries generated 45 percent of labor earnings, in contrast to the 50 percent recorded during the war (Bureau of Economic Analysis 2000).

9. Under Census Bureau definitions, the urban population is different from and larger than the population living in metropolitan areas; as we use the term here, the urbanization rate refers to the percentage of the population living in metropolitan areas. The Census Bureau definition of an urban area is any settlement with more than 2,500 people. A metropolitan statistical area (MSA), on the other hand, has a core urban area of at least 50,000. The definition of an urban area we use in this book corresponds to that of a "large urban area" in Census Bureau terminology.

10. These figures refer to the growth of cities that were already classified as metropolitan areas in 1978. However, the metropolitan area population also expanded because

several small cities—Missoula, Montana, and Pocatello, Idaho, to name just two—
grew enough between 1978 and 1998 to be classified as metropolitan areas. If the
growth of these cities is included in the calculation, the metropolitan and non-metropolitan populations grew by 100 percent and 8 percent, respectively.

11. For the region as a whole, including metropolitan areas, the decline was from about
9 to 3 percent. Note that because of the level of aggregation in the Regional Economic
Information System data from which these figures were calculated, we have no
measure of employment in wood products and metal smelting and refining for non-
metropolitan areas. Thus, these industries are not included in the natural resource
sector in this discussion.

CHAPTER 4

Converting "Good" Jobs
to "Lousy" Jobs?

The Effect of Changes
in Industrial Structure
on Wages and Well-Being

In the early 1980s, the copper mining and smelting complex that had operated for more than a century in the Butte-Anaconda area of Montana shut down, resulting in the layoff of thousands of workers. Less than a decade earlier, the Anaconda Copper Mining Company's operations in these communities had been estimated to represent almost three-quarters of the area's economic base. But in the interim, the company disappeared in a corporate takeover and its facilities were abandoned.

Economic redevelopment efforts in the area focused in part on promoting new recreation and tourism attractions. A high-altitude sports center, including an Olympic-standard speed skating facility, was built in Butte. Army National Guard helicopters lifted a ninety-foot-tall, gleaming white statue titled *Our Lady of the Rockies* to a mountain peak overlooking the city. Visitors were directed to a viewing platform at the gigantic Berkeley Pit, which was slowly filling with shimmering, turquoise water, a toxic brew of mining wastes. And on the tailings piles adjacent to the old smelter in the town of Anaconda, a Jack Nicklaus–designed golf course was constructed as part of the reclamation effort.

These dramatic changes—the closing of the mine and smelter and the opening of tourism and recreation facilities—did not simply mean that Butte was losing its historical place as a copper producer. Rather, they appeared also to mean that miners and smelter workers would have to give up the highest-paid blue-collar work in Montana for jobs passing out gym towels, grooming putting greens, or selling plastic rosaries and soft drinks to tourists. And it was not just in Montana that this was happening. Nor was it just in the copper industry. The copper, silver, uranium, coal, oil, natural gas, timber, ranching, and farming industries all seemed to be discarding workers, who then had to scramble desperately for whatever alternative work was to be found. Workers in communities that depended on these natural resource industries appeared to be in for hard times indeed.

For most residents of the Mountain West, the decline in pay across the region since the late 1970s is a clear sign that their economy is failing them. And the cause of this failure seems obvious. If pay is falling, it must be because local employment opportunities are deteriorating; in the popular phrasing, good jobs are disappearing and lousy jobs are replacing them. Just what to do about it is also pretty obvious: since the area needs better jobs, public policy must focus on attracting firms that pay wages well above those currently available. Industrial recruitment campaigns, tax breaks, publicly funded industrial parks, and other improvements in the local "business climate" are in order so that high-wage firms will find the local area a profitable place to set up shop.

At the national level, Barry Bluestone and Bennett Harrison labeled the process of replacing high-wage jobs with low-wage jobs "deindustrialization." Their 1982 book, *The Deindustrialization of America: Plant Closings, Community Abandonment, and the Dismantling of Basic Industry,* lays out the story: it is the loss of the country's industrial capacity as factories relocate to lower-wage areas in the United States or overseas that drives wages downward:

> What people seem to be feeling . . . is a deepening sense of *insecurity,* growing out of the collapse all around them of the traditional economic base of their communities. Their very jobs are being pulled out from under them. And instead of providing new employment opportunities, a higher standard of living, and enhanced security, the decisions of corporate managers are doing just the opposite. . . . Deindustrialization is occurring—on a surprisingly massive scale. It can be seen from North to South and East to West. It is happening as the largest, most powerful corporations in the nation shut down older plants in the industrial heartland . . . to move to new industrial zones . . . and overseas. (Bluestone and Harrison 1982, pp. 46–47)

There is little doubt that in the Mountain West, the decline in employment in natural resource industries since the late 1970s has triggered similar feelings of economic insecurity. At the state and local levels, environmental regulations, business taxes, and other public policies are said to burden firms in high-wage industries, destroying good jobs and replacing them with poorly paid ones in such industries as services, trade, and tourism. At the federal level, at which the government controls extensive public lands and manages many hydroelectric and irrigation projects in the region, resource management policies are widely believed to shape the fortunes of local natural resource industries. Because these industries have been viewed historically as the engines driving local economic activity, advocates of natural resource development often claim that federal policies aimed at better protecting environmental values are undermining the local economy and destroying good jobs.

This interpretation of events in the local economy focuses on the structure, *by industry,* of local employment opportunities. Low wages or incomes are explained by the existence of an inferior mix of jobs, with too many jobs in industries that pay badly and too few jobs in industries that pay well. In this view, the shift in jobs toward industries that pay badly is the fundamental cause of the falling average earnings of all workers; given the facts, this proposition seems like little more than common sense.

In chapters 2 and 3, we described the behavior of real pay per job and the changes in industrial structure that took place in the Mountain West over the last two decades or so of the twentieth century. Setting aside the details, the essential findings in those chapters were that at the same time jobs in the natural resource industries and other goods-producing industries began to disappear and be replaced by jobs in services, retail trade, and other non-goods-producing industries, real earnings per job fell sharply and never really recovered. The inescapable conclusion seems to be that these two developments did not just happen to occur at the same time but were cause and effect.

In this chapter, however, we present more detailed analyses of several kinds of data and conclude that shifts in industrial structure were responsible for at most only a small part of the dramatic changes that occurred during this period in the level and distribution of wages in the Mountain West. Although this finding contradicts the conventional wisdom in the region, numerous studies of different groups of workers and different time periods have reached similar conclusions for other geographic areas. We wrap up the chapter with a discussion of why that might be the case.

We also discuss how the changes in the industrial structure of employment have affected individual workers over time. Examining individual wage histories, we trace the effects of these economic shifts on the stability of employment, the types of industrial shifts workers actually made, and the changes in wages that accompanied those shifts. We find that individual workers experienced considerable stability in employment. Very few shifted between industries, and those who did, on average, saw their wages rise. The very small percentage of workers shifting out of the natural resource sector saw slight declines in their wages but retained most of the above-average earnings associated with their previous employment. In particular, workers leaving relatively highly paid industries did not, in general, take low-paying jobs in tourism or retail trade. The combination of these results suggests that changes in the structure of the economy did not force damaging job changes on most individual workers.

INDUSTRIAL STRUCTURE AND PAY LEVELS

In analyzing the relationship between economic structure and pay, it is critical to recognize the fact that for workers with given levels of skill, experience, and education, pay differs substantially from one industry to another. Almost all workers in a paper mill, for example, will be paid significantly more than their counterparts in a textile plant. It is this fact that lies behind the concept of "good" jobs and "lousy" jobs; how good (or bad) a job is depends on the industry in which it is based.[1]

In the context of competitive labor markets, economists find it hard to explain such substantial and persistent differences in the rewards for labor of apparently equivalent quality. In a simple theoretical world where workers compete for jobs, employers compete for workers, and the goods produced are sold in competitive markets, such differences should disappear. Workers of equal skill and experience should be paid the same no matter what industry employs them.[2] But there is clear evidence that they are not.

When differences in skill, education, experience, occupation, sex, race, marital status, union membership, and so forth within the workforce are accounted for, there are still significant wage differences in different industries (Krueger and Summers 1988). Workers in mining, metal refining and smelting, chemicals, communications, and public utilities earn wages 25 to 35 percent above the average for all workers with similar personal characteristics. On the other hand, workers in eating and drinking establishments, other retail activities, entertainment, and educational services earn 15 to 20 percent less than the average for all other similarly qualified workers. The extremes are even greater than these examples suggest. Petroleum workers earn 62 percent more than the average, whereas private household service workers earn 52 percent less (Krueger and Summers 1988, table 2). These differences in wages among different industries are persistent and existed for most of the twentieth century (Krueger and Summers 1986).

The fact is that certain industries pay a wage "premium"—an amount above what the competitive market usually pays for equivalent workers.[3] This economic reality lays the basis for the structural view of the determinants of local wages: wage payments depend on the local industrial mix, happenstance, and luck. When workers happen to live in a place where firms providing high-premium jobs are located and are lucky enough to get those jobs, their earnings are much higher than those of workers with similar qualifications who live where such high-premium jobs are not available or who are unlucky enough to miss out on the ones that are. In this context, the appropriate public economic policy to raise local wages is to recruit firms that pay such wage premiums.

THE IMPORTANCE OF *ACCESSIBLE* HIGH-WAGE JOBS

Although the kinds of jobs available to workers and the premiums they pay play an important role in determining wages, so do skill, education, experience, and other worker characteristics. This is because not all jobs are accessible to all workers; skill *does* matter. Even with all the luck in the world, salesclerks will not suddenly find themselves working as heart surgeons. But in the structural view, in explaining the differences we observe in workers' earnings, skills may not matter as much as the wage premiums paid to workers of equivalent potential productivity. Two high school graduates with ten years of work experience may indeed be equally qualified. But if one works in an automobile assembly plant and the other in a nursing home, their earnings will be quite different.

What efforts to promote high-wage job growth can accomplish depends critically on why the new jobs pay higher wages. If local workers who currently hold poorly paid jobs do not have the qualifications they need to take the new, better jobs that have become available, evidently those new jobs must be filled by qualified workers who move into the community. This will be of little benefit to existing low-wage workers, even though there may be gratifying evidence of rising average earnings, which can happen when the relatively high pay of new residents is taken into account.[4]

DOES CHANGING INDUSTRIAL STRUCTURE EXPLAIN DECLINING PAY? THE EMPIRICAL EVIDENCE

Although it is possible for changes in industrial structure to reduce wages, it is important to understand that earnings can fall for other reasons, including growing international competition, the introduction of laborsaving technologies, and declining union influence. This makes sorting out and isolating the effect of structural change on wages a complex task. It also suggests the possibility that quantitatively, structural change just may not be very important; in the final analysis, other factors may explain the bulk of wage developments.

In fact, many careful empirical analyses carried out during the 1990s at the national, regional, and state levels have addressed this issue, and all have shown that changes in the way jobs are distributed among industries can explain very little of the decline in pay.

Analyzing the Structure-Wage Link Nationally

Over time, wage levels rise or fall not only because of changing industrial structure but also because workers' characteristics (age, educational attainment, union membership, and so forth) and the value the labor market puts on those characteristics change as well. To isolate the effect of changing industrial structure, it is necessary to control for these other influences statistically. Numerous studies have done that.

In one such study, John Bound and George Johnson (1992) employed national data spanning the 1980s, when pay declined in many regions and pay inequality increased. They found that shifts in the industrial structure of employment had less than a 1 percent effect on the relative hourly wages[5] of various demographic groups of workers. In general, less than 10 percent of the total change in a demographic group's relative wage during the 1980s could be attributed to changes in the industrial distribution of employment.

Other analyses of national data have led to similar conclusions. Kevin Murphy and Finis Welch (1993) found that between 1978 and 1989, when the average real wages of all workers declined by 4 percent, shifts in employment between industries could explain only about one-eighth of the decline in men's wages and none of the change in women's wages. The average annual wage for men fell by $1,200 between 1978 and 1989—from $30,000 to $28,800 in 1999 dollars—but the change in industrial structure was responsible for only about $144 of this decline.[6] The results were the same for more narrowly defined groups of workers. During this period, for example, the wages of workers who did not finish high school declined by 14 percent while those of college graduates rose by 8 percent. But only one-fifth to one-third of these changes could be explained in terms of shifts in employment opportunities among industries (Murphy and Welch 1993, p. 113). For instance, a worker who did not finish high school earned about $23,000 per year in 1978 (again expressed in 1999 dollars). Between 1978 and 1989, this wage declined by about $3,200, and about $800 of this decline was caused by the shift in employment from higher- to lower-wage industries.

Even the broad shift in employment from goods production to services, often considered the culprit behind real wage stagnation, has been shown to account for less than 15 percent of the change in the overall level of wages and wage inequality; the effect of this structural shift on the wages of workers in the bottom 50 percent of the workforce is somewhat greater but still very small (Juhn, Murphy, and Pierce 1993, p. 413).

The effect of structural change on the *distribution* of wages appears to be equally modest. Robert Valletta (1997, p. 28) estimated what the full distribution of wages would have been in 1995 if the industrial composition of employment had been frozen as it was in the late 1970s but the personal productive characteristics of workers had continued to develop as they actually did through the mid-1990s. When this hypothetical distribution was compared with its actual counterpart, there was almost no discernible difference. Changes in industrial structure explained only about 10 percent of the decline in the average wage and only about 5 percent of the increase in wage inequality.

At the regional level, Neil Templeton (1998) analyzed changes in Pacific Northwest hourly wages between two time periods, 1977–1981 and 1988–1993. In the interval between these periods, wages fell sharply across the board. In the Pacific Northwest, wages for young, less educated workers plunged by 20 to 25 percent while overall wages stagnated. It was also during this interval that timber, mining, and metal smelting employment plummeted in the region.

Following Bound and Johnson (1992), Templeton estimated the effect on mean hourly wages of changes in the industrial and occupational composition of employment and in the education, experience, and other personal characteristics of the workforce, so that the effect of changes in industrial structure could be identified and isolated. For all the various groups defined by age, education, and gender, such changes in industrial structure had at most very small negative effects on hourly wages; for no group did the structural effect cause more than a 2 percent decline. For younger, less educated workers, who suffered the largest wage declines (20 to 25 percent, depending on gender), only one-tenth to one-fifth of the decline could be explained by industrial shifts in employment (Templeton 1998, tables 4.5, 4.13).

Testing the Structural Hypothesis in the Mountain West
Evidence from the United States as a whole and the Pacific Northwest in particular suggests that structural change is responsible for relatively little wage change. But the same need not be true of the Mountain West, where arguably the pattern of structural change has been different and more profound. Unlike the rest of the country, the region has historically been heavily dependent on natural resource industries, and these industries declined dramatically in relative and absolute terms over the last two decades of the twentieth century.

During the 1980s, employment in the natural resource industries of the

Mountain West, including farming, ranching, mining, metal smelting, and lumber, plummeted, as, of course, did earnings per job (see figures 2.1, 3.1, and 3.2). Is it not possible that this particularly sharp decline in very high wage industries, on which the region especially depended, played a much bigger role in driving down wages than was the case in the rest of the country?[7]

To answer this question, we can "decompose" the observed decline in the economy-wide average pay per job, that is, divide it into two components that measure, respectively, the decline in the average that would have occurred if (1) pay in each job had been held constant but workers had moved from high- to low-paid jobs as they actually did or, alternatively, (2) workers had not changed jobs but pay in all jobs had fallen as it actually did.[8] The first of these components measures the effect on wages of changing industrial structure; it tells us what would have happened to average pay per job if the structure of employment had changed but pay per job in each industry had been frozen.[9] The second component measures how much average pay per job fell because pay per job in all industries was changing; it tells us how much average pay per job would have fallen even if the structure of employment had been frozen.[10]

Table 4.1 reports the results of two such decompositions of the change in average pay per job in the Mountain West. In these decompositions, we divided the economy into two sectors, which between them account for all employment. The two decompositions differ from each other in the way the two sectors used to describe the structure of the economy are specified. In the first, the two sectors are natural resources and all other non-farm economic activities (labeled "Rest of the Economy"); over the period 1978–1988, natural resource employment fell both in absolute numbers and as a share of the total. In the second decomposition, the two sectors consist of goods production and non-goods production; over the period, employment in goods production rose in absolute numbers but fell as a share of the total.

The period analyzed is 1978–1988 because it was during that time average pay per job declined precipitously. From 1988 to 1998 it rose, recovering much of the ground lost during the previous decade, and by 1998 it was just 3.4 percent below what it had been twenty years earlier.[11]

The table shows 1978 pay per job and share of total employment by sector and for the economy as a whole, as well as the changes in pay per job and employment shares that took place over the period. These values were used to calculate the percentage of actual decline in average pay per job that would have occurred even if the share of employment in the high-wage sector had never fallen after 1978.

We can illustrate this calculation using the figures from the section of the table labeled "Sector Composition: Natural Resources and the Rest of the Econ-

Table 4.1. Sources of Declining Real Pay per Job in the Mountain West, 1978–1988 (1998 Dollars)

Economic Sectors	1978 Employment Share	1978–1988 Change in Employment Share	1978 Pay per Job	1978–1988 Change in Pay per Job	Percentage Loss in Pay per Job with No Employment Shift
Sector Composition: Natural Resources and the Rest of the Economy					
Natural resources	8.0%	–2.7%	$35,578	–$5,513	
Rest of the economy	92.0%	2.7%	$28,133	–$2,316	
Total economy	100.0%	0.0%	$28,732	–$2,689	**96%**
Sector Composition: Goods-Producing and Non-Goods-Producing					
Goods-producing	24.2%	4.1%	$36,832	–$4,005	
Non-goods-producing	75.8%	–4.1%	$26,146	–$1,815	
Total economy	100.0%	0.0%	$28,732	–$2,689	**87%**

Source: Computed by the authors using data from Bureau of Economic Analysis 1999.

omy." Suppose the shares of employment in the natural resource sector and in the rest of the economy had remained at their 1978 levels, 8 percent and 92 percent, respectively. Suppose as well that the levels of pay per job in the natural resource sector and in the rest of the economy had fallen as they actually did between 1978 and 1988, by $5,513 and $2,316, respectively. In this case, the decline in average pay for all jobs would have been $2,572,[12] which is 96 percent of the $2,689 decline that actually occurred.

For the natural resource sector to have retained the same share of total employment, it would have had to expand by 35 percent instead of declining by 11 percent. Even if this highly implausible reversal of actual employment trends had taken place, almost all the decline in average real pay per job would have occurred anyway.

Similarly, if, rather than lagging behind the rest of the economy, goods production had expanded rapidly enough to maintain its share of total employment, 87 percent of the fall in average pay per job would have occurred anyway. That is, almost all the actual decline would have taken place even if goods production had expanded three times as fast as it actually did, by 35 percent instead of 13 percent.

The reason declining employment in natural resources or goods production played such a small part in the fall in average pay per job is that pay was declining everywhere, and particularly sharply in natural resources and goods production. In fact, as figure 4.1 illustrates, pay per job was falling much more rapidly in goods-producing than in non-goods-producing industries.

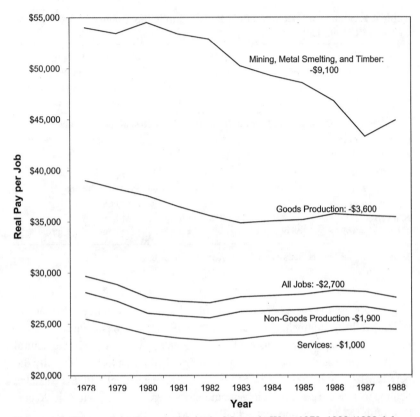

FIGURE 4.1. Changes in real pay per job in the Mountain West, 1978–1988 (1998 dollars). Declining pay per job was most pronounced in (non-agricultural) natural resource industries and goods production in general. *Source:* Bureau of Economic Analysis 1999.

Compared with the situation in non-goods-producing industries, between 1978 and 1988 real pay per job fell five times as far in natural resource industries and twice as far in goods-producing industries in general. It was these large declines in pay per job in *all* industries, led by natural resources and goods, that drove almost all the fall in average pay, not a shift in employment from high- to low-wage industries.[13]

Analyzing the Effect of Structural Change in One State: Montana

In terms of declining average pay per job, Montana led the Mountain West. Although real pay per job across the region fell by 10 percent between 1978 and 1988, in Montana the decline was twice as great. And between 1988 and

1998, when real pay per job recovered across the region, in Montana it continued to deteriorate.

The distinctive structure of Montana's economy serves as a backdrop for this particularly steep fall in pay. In 1996, Montana was the least metropolitan state not only in the Mountain West but also in the country as a whole. Lacking metropolitan centers like Denver, Phoenix, Salt Lake City, Albuquerque, or Boise, with their diverse collection of trade, service, and manufacturing activities, Montana was more than twice as dependent as the region as a whole on its natural resource industries, and it was presumably more vulnerable when these industries fell on hard times.

And hard times there were. During the 1980s, copper mining and smelting and oil and gas exploration nearly shut down in the state, causing thousands of workers to be laid off. The wood products industry entered an extended depression, during which advances in technology permanently displaced thousands of workers. And agriculture suffered from both low prices and droughts. Even if there is evidence that earnings in the Mountain West were not much affected by adverse structural change, things might have been different in Montana, where natural resource dependence was substantially greater and the distress of natural resource industries more pronounced. Was the rapidly changing structure of the state's economy responsible for its dubious distinction in claiming the region's lowest pay?

Table 4.2 reports the results of three decompositions of the decline in average pay per job in Montana during the period 1978–1988; the interpretation of the table is identical to that of table 4.1. In the first decomposition in table 4.2, the two sectors are non-farm goods production and all other economic activities; over the ten-year period, employment shifted from the former to the latter.[14] In the second decomposition, the sectors consist of services,[15] the expansion of which has given rise to the notion of an emergent "service economy," and all other economic activities. Over the period, the share of employment in services rose. In the final decomposition, the sectors are the aggregate of those high-wage industries that declined in Montana during the 1980s and all other activities.[16] The industries making up this high-wage sector included metal mining and smelting, logging and wood products, oil and gas exploration, heavy construction, and railroads. We grouped these industries together not because they produce similar products but rather to "stack the deck" in favor of the structural interpretation of falling pay.

The results reported in table 4.2 demonstrate that however the sectors are defined, employment shifted from higher- to lower-paid sectors. But more important, even if the share of workers employed in the higher-wage sector (however it is defined) had not declined *at all,* 90 to 98 percent of the substantial fall

Table 4.2. Sources of Declining Real Pay per Job in Montana, 1978–1988 (1998 Dollars)

Economic Sectors	1978 Employment Share	1978–1988 Change in Employment Share	1978 Pay per Job	1978–1988 Change in Pay per Job	Percentage Loss in Pay per Job with No Employment Shift
Sector Composition: Non-Farm Goods Production and the Rest of the Economy					
Non-Farm Goods Production	18.3%	–3.7%	$39,203	–$9,648	
Rest of the economy	81.7%	3.7%	$24,670	–$3,525	
Total Economy	100.0%	0.0%	$27,331	–$4,956	94%
Sector Composition: Services and the Rest of the Economy					
Services	21.1%	5.5%	$21,061	–$2,100	
Rest of the Economy	78.9%	–5.5%	$28,733	–$7,053	
Total Economy	100.0%	0.0%	$27,114	–$6,157	98%
Sector Composition: Declining High-Wage Sectors and the Rest of the Economy					
Declining High-Wage Sectors	8.6%	–4.1%	$44,883	–$8,943	
Rest of the Economy	91.4%	4.1%	$25,439	–$5,480	
Total Economy	100.0%	0.0%	$27,114	–$6,428	90%

Source: Computed by the authors using data from Bureau of Economic Analysis 1999.

in average pay per job would have taken place. As in the Mountain West as a whole, the dominant source of declining pay was not shifts in employment from high- to low-wage industries but an across-the-board decrease in pay, including large decreases in pay in the high-wage sectors.

The period between 1978 and 1988 is of particular interest because that was when most of Montana's decline in pay took place. But for the longer time period 1978–1998, the results are the same; if employment had not shifted from goods to non-goods production, 94 percent of the decline in pay per job would have taken place anyway. Even more dramatic: if, instead of losing 10,000 high-wage jobs, Montana had *gained* 10,000 new ones, so that in 1998 the proportion of high-wage goods-producing jobs was no less than in 1978, 84 percent of the decline in pay per job would still have taken place.

Cutting Things More Finely: Looking More Closely at Industrial Structure

In analyzing the effect of the change in industrial structure in the Mountain West and in Montana, we somewhat arbitrarily divided the economy into sets of just two sectors—goods- and non-goods-producing, natural resources and the rest of the economy, high-wage and other, and so forth. In discussions of structural change, economic activities are often dichotomized in this way; in this setting, structural change consists of the expansion of one sector at the expense of the other. But this is obviously a simplification. Bifurcating the economy in this way ignores shifts in employment taking place *within* both the goods-producing and non-goods-producing sectors; such intrasectoral realignments of employment could have important effects. For instance, if high-wage mining jobs are replaced with minimum-wage food-processing jobs, total employment in goods production will be unchanged. Similarly, if skilled nursing jobs are replaced with relatively unskilled hotel jobs, total employment in non–goods production will be unchanged. In this case, there would appear to be no structural change taking place because these employment shifts would occur entirely within the large sectors into which the economy has been artificially divided. Instead, pay per job would appear to decline in both goods and non-goods production, leading to the incorrect conclusion that structural change played no role in falling average earnings.

Some of the more important changes in the distribution of employment in Montana between 1976 and 1996 that took place *within* the dichotomous sectors reported on in table 4.2 include the following:

- The loss of 2,888 jobs in wood products and metal smelting and the gain of 5,000 jobs in other durable manufacturing sectors
- The loss of 5,400 jobs in farming and the gain of 5,500 jobs in agricultural services
- The loss of 2,500 jobs in the federal government and the gain of 14,000 jobs in state and local government
- The loss of 1,100 jobs in food processing and the gain of 2,500 jobs in other non-durable manufacturing
- The loss of 3,300 jobs in railroads and the gain of 7,400 jobs in other transportation industries

We can avoid obscuring these important shifts in the structure of employment if, instead of aggregating all activities into two broad sectors, we account separately for *all* job shifts among approximately seventy narrowly defined industries. This allows estimation of the effect on pay per job of such employment shifts *within* the larger dichotomous sectors employed previously. Such an analysis of the Montana economy reveals that the effect of structural change on earnings was greater than that reported in table 4.2. However, even these more detailed changes in industrial structure explain only a fraction, about 20 percent, of changes in average pay per job. Put the other way, 80 percent of the decline would have taken place even if there had been no change in the distribution of jobs among this much larger and more diverse collection of industries.[17]

Clearly, there have been significant shifts in employment that do not fall into the "goods to services" dichotomy. Most of the shifts just listed involved movement from higher- to lower-paying jobs. At the same time, however, pay levels were dropping in almost all sectors. It is these declines in pay, which happened with almost no regard for the industry in which a worker was employed, that explain the bulk of the fall in average pay per job, rather than shifts in the distribution of employment among industries.

Structural Change in the Timber-Dependent Pacific Northwest

If the structural explanation of falling pay is applicable anywhere, it should be in poorly diversified local economies that historically have been heavily dependent on a particular industry that has recently been in relative or absolute decline. In the Pacific Northwest, timber-dependent areas provide examples of such economies; southwestern Oregon is one such example.

In the six-county area in the southwestern corner of the state, 27 percent of total earnings were derived from the wood products industry in 1978. Among the six counties, this percentage ranged from a low of 17 to a high of 37. Total earnings in lumber and wood products declined by almost 25 percent between 1978 and 1988 and by 43 percent between 1978 and 1998. And average annual real pay per job in the area declined by $6,700 between 1978 and 1998.

Even in this case of extreme dependence, however, the collapse in average pay per job during the 1980s was led by even sharper reductions *within* the wood products industry, rather than by shifts of employment out of wood products. Real annual pay per job in wood products declined by $8,300 while pay per job in the rest of the economy declined by $4,200 per year. Employment in wood products actually rose, although its share of total employment declined by 2.5 percentage points. Decomposition analysis indicates that had there been no decline in wood products' share of total employment (that is, if employment in wood products had actually increased significantly with the rest of the economy), 93 percent of the decline in average real pay would have taken place anyway.

This analysis can be extended to all forty-five timber-dependent counties in the Pacific Northwest states, including those in northern California, western and eastern Washington, northern Idaho, and western Montana as well as southwestern Oregon.[18] Between 1976 and 1996, average real pay per job in these timber-dependent counties fell by $6,500. However, if the share of employment in the goods-producing sector, which was heavily dominated by the wood products industry in these counties, had been frozen at its 1976 level, 95 percent of this decline would have taken place anyway.[19] That is because real annual pay per job plummeted by $10,400 in goods production but fell by "only" $3,900 in non-goods-producing industries. In 1976, jobs in the goods-producing sector paid $8,000 per year more, and those in the non-goods-producing sector paid $4,000 per year less, than the average. But by 1996, pay was only $3,000 above average in the goods-producing sector and only $1,000 below average in non–goods production. It was becoming harder to distinguish the "good" jobs from the "lousy" jobs.

There is no mystery regarding what happened to pay in the wood products industry in the Pacific Northwest during the early 1980s. The twin back-to-back recessions at the beginning of the decade, combined with 14 percent mortgage rates, led to a dramatic decline in home building and other construction across the country. National housing starts in 1981 were half those in 1978. This reduced the demand for building materials, including lumber. Lumber mills scaled back production or shut down. In the highly unionized wood products industry in the Pacific Northwest, owners responded to these pressures on their profits by unilaterally abrogating existing collective bargaining agreements and imposing significant pay reductions (Widenor 1991). The unions resisted, but mill owners had the superior bargaining position, and the pay reductions held. The severe downward pressure on pay was felt even in "good" jobs.

STRUCTURE AND RELATIVE PAY LEVELS IN MONTANA

In the preceding sections, we examined the relationship between changing economic structure and the *decline* in pay that occurred in various geographic settings over approximately the last twenty years of the twentieth century. In every case, the conclusion is the same: although they occurred at about the same time, structural change did not cause the fall in wages. But a different question is this: regardless of why they might have fallen, could Mountain West wages not be lower than those in the rest of the country because of structural factors? In other words, might not workers in the region earn less than their counterparts elsewhere simply because the mix of jobs available to them is not as good?

Although a particularly bad job mix might explain the region's wage disadvantage, other factors could also be important. Workers in the Mountain West might have inferior qualifications, or their qualifications might be less generously rewarded in regional labor markets. It is also possible that even if the distribution of employment between high- and low-wage industries was similar to that in the country as a whole, all regional pay premiums could be low by national standards.

To sort out these separate influences in the case of Montana, we analyzed, for both the state and the country as a whole, the relationship between the hourly pay of individual workers and the personal characteristics—education, age, occupation, industry, and the like—believed to be important in determining that pay.[20] A comparison of these relationships at the state and national levels allows us to estimate how much of the state's wage shortfall would have disappeared if (1) the qualifications of Montana workers had been rewarded as well in the state as elsewhere and (2) industries in the state had paid the same wage premiums as their national counterparts. We can also determine what portion of the remaining shortfall, if any, would then have been attributable to Montana workers either having inferior qualifications or working in industries with particularly low pay.

In the first half of the 1990s, the hourly wages received by Montana workers were 13.7 percent below the national average. Of this difference, less than one-fifth—2.5 percentage points—was due to differences between Montana and the rest of the country in the distribution of employment between low- and high-wage industries. Inferior personal qualifications had even less to do with relatively low wages; in fact, in terms of years of schooling, workers in Montana were somewhat better qualified than workers elsewhere. The most important factors explaining the state's relatively low wages were inferior rewards for valuable personal characteristics such as education and low wage premiums across all industries. In other words, the state's problem was not that it lacked the kinds of jobs normally considered to be good in the American economy. The problem was that in Montana, even "good" jobs were not that good.

THE INDIVIDUAL LABOR MARKET EXPERIENCES OF WORKERS CHANGING JOBS

Up to this point, we have analyzed the behavior over time of *average* earnings for large groups of workers. Averages are helpful; they provide some sense of what is "typical" for a group. But they can also be misleading because many, even most, individual members can have personal experiences that are not at all average.

In our research on the changing structure of employment opportunities in the Mountain West,[21] we tracked the employment histories of hundreds of thousands of individual workers so that we could understand the actual job changes they were experiencing and the consequences of those changes on their pay. With so many workers to report on, we had no choice but to use summary statistics such as averages to report our results in the pages that follow. However, to lend a little bit of flesh and blood to what these summary statistics tell us, we begin with a few examples of some of the more important transitions individual workers were making.

Consider any one of the urban trade centers in Mountain West states that are surrounded by forests—examples are Coeur d'Alene, Idaho; Kalispell, Missoula, or Bozeman, Montana; Sheridan, Wyoming; Flagstaff, Arizona; and Durango, Colorado. Lumber and wood products were once important industries in those areas, but over the last three decades of the twentieth century, technological change allowed mills to operate with smaller and smaller workforces, and those that could not afford to modernize were slowly shut down. Meanwhile, as these centers grew rapidly, employment in almost every other industry increased. Some activities—construction, tourism-related trade and services, retail trade, business services, and medical care—provided for the bulk of new jobs. Others—finance, education, public utilities, and transportation, for example—played a smaller role. The mix of employment opportunities in these communities was changing rapidly, and it seemed almost self-evident that to match these changes, many workers were being pushed from one industry to another, usually to their detriment. After all, if average earnings were declining, well-paid jobs in the woods and mills were disappearing, and lousy jobs in trade and services were cropping up everywhere, was it not just about inevitable that workers were moving from good to bad jobs? As it turns out, such job changes were not really all that common.

For one thing, most workers did not change jobs at all. This was possible because the changes occurring in the mix of employment opportunities, sweeping as they appeared to be, could generally be accommodated by normal attrition and labor force growth. With retirements and the normal turnover that occurs as workers move away, go to school, or find more attractive jobs, significant downsizing of an industry such as the wood products industry can take place with few forced layoffs. At the same time, industries that are expanding rapidly do not have to attract workers from other parts of the local economy; instead, they can draw on new entrants into the labor force—young workers just leaving school, older adults returning to employment, and in-migrants.

Some workers, of course, did leave the shrinking lumber and wood products industries—either voluntarily or otherwise—and seek work elsewhere. Some ended up in low-wage retail trade and tourism-related jobs. But many, relying on their skills and industrial work experience, found their way into relatively well-paid jobs in construction, manufacturing, and transportation and were able to maintain their earnings.

In general, older, long-term workers' jobs were protected by seniority as companies reduced their workforces, and the younger, more mobile and flexible workers made the employment adjustments. Since young workers tend to change jobs frequently anyway, the degree of disruption in workers' lives was not as great as it otherwise might have been.

It was not workers leaving the wood products industry, then, who filled the growing number of poorly paid jobs in trade and services. Instead, these jobs were taken mainly by new workers with limited experience and skill: high school graduates, college students, women reentering the workforce, and so forth. As these workers gained experience and skills or finished their schooling, they left those jobs for higher-paying ones in other industries. Low-wage jobs were the base from which many workers launched themselves on rising career paths.

Additional highly paid technical and professional jobs in industries such as medical care and business services were also filled by new workers—recent college and professional school graduates and highly trained and experienced in-migrants—physicians, business consultants, and others who valued the quality of life in the region as well as the opportunity to earn an ample income.

In an environment, then, in which job opportunities appeared to be deteriorating and average earnings were declining, many workers were making surprisingly positive transitions—from a declining high-wage industry to a growing one; from first-time employment in a low-wage industry to higher earnings elsewhere; from education to work; and from employment elsewhere to a job within the region.

Interpreting Summary Statistics

When the average earnings of a group of workers are falling, it is tempting to conclude that most members of that group are experiencing declining pay individually as well. But surprisingly, such a conclusion is not warranted. Partly, this is true simply because some workers are earning more and others less, and the movement of the average does not tell us how many fall into each category.

Even more significantly, average pay in any given year reflects the experience of the workers who were active in the labor market *that year*. Each year, individuals in the workforce change as a result of in- and out-migration, retirement, and the entry of new workers. New entrants into the workforce typically are relatively young and inexperienced and therefore tend to earn lower wages than other workers. If many new workers are coming into the workforce, average pay could decline even though most workers' earnings are actually rising, with new workers moving from zero to whatever low starting wage they earn and other workers receiving the pay increases normally associated with additional experience.[22]

Similarly, a shift in the distribution of workers among industries—say, a declining share in natural resources and a rising share in tourism[23]—does not necessarily tell us much about the kind of job changes individuals are actually experiencing. In particular, using the same example, it does not mean that natural resource workers are necessarily moving into tourism. The natural resource industries' share of employment could shrink not because workers are being laid off but because the industry is growing more slowly than the overall economy. Meanwhile, new entrants into the workforce could be staffing the new tourism jobs.

Public concern about the changing structure of employment often centers on the fear that those changes have eroded the economic status of individual workers. If good jobs are being lost and poorer-quality jobs are replacing them, it appears inevitable that workers who have become attached to good jobs in particular industries are being forced out of those industries and into unemployment, lower-paid employment, a series of unstable jobs, or multiple jobs. After all, what else could be happening to workers in declining high-wage industries?

Because it involves keeping track of the same workers over many years, it is not easy to trace the actual labor market experiences of individual workers as they change jobs. In general, federal labor statistics do not allow such tracking.[24] Therefore, to obtain long-term histories of individual workers, we made use of one state's (Montana's) unemployment insurance database. Using this source, we were able to construct quarterly wage histories of individual workers for the period 1988 to 1996. These histories show the amount the worker earned and the industry or industries in which he or she was employed in each of the thirty-six quarters of this nine-year period. Since some workers either entered or left employment or both during the period, many histories show quarters in which there are no earnings. In all cases, the data refer only to employment that was "covered," that is, covered by Montana unemployment insurance.[25]

We studied only those workers who were in covered employment for at least two years. This means that all the workers in our sample could potentially have become "attached" to a particular industry, with attachment defined as the completion of eight quarters of continuous employment in that industry alone. Moreover, since we wanted to trace what happened to workers for at least the three-year period following attachment, we limited our analysis to those workers who completed two years of employment prior to the first quarter of 1994, three years before the end of our sample period. From all the employment histories at our disposal, we were able to extract those of about 250,000 workers who met these requirements.[26] The distribution of these workers across industries closely matched the distribution of total employment in Montana in 1996.

The Stability of Employment

Most workers become attached to a particular industry relatively rapidly. Of workers with employment histories of eight or more quarters, 86 percent became attached at some point in their work history. On average, it took workers only a little more than a year (5.3 quarters) after entering covered employment to find a job in the industry to which the worker then became attached. The 14 percent of workers who did not make such an attachment fared much more poorly than those who did. Earnings of attached workers were twice those of unattached workers. Those who failed to become attached to an industry had wages that were 40 percent below the average.

Just as most workers became attached to a particular industry, after becoming attached to an industry most workers stayed in it well beyond two years. Three years after becoming attached, 64 percent were still in the same industry. Another 16 percent stayed in the industry but left covered employment less than three years after becoming attached. Thus, 80 percent of attached workers remained in the same industry for the full follow-up period or for as long as they could be tracked. Only 17 percent of attached workers ended the follow-up period in an industry different from the one to which they originally became attached.

The finding that a high proportion of workers became attached to a single industry relatively quickly, and then remained so, points to considerable stability in employment among workers in the late 1980s and the first half of the 1990s, despite considerable structural change in overall employment in Montana. In other words, structural change did not disrupt the employment experiences of most workers. This should not be entirely surprising. To the extent that it occurs slowly enough to be accommodated by normal employment turnover and the entry of new workers into the workforce, structural change need not impose a burden on existing attached workers.

Attached Workers Who Changed Industries

Despite the prevalence of persistent attachment to a single industry, 17 percent of attached workers did change industries. Which industries did they leave, and to which industries did they move? How did they fare in terms of pay? Does their experience reinforce the fear that the shifting structure of employment displaced workers, forcing them out of good jobs in natural resources and goods production and into the lower-paid but expanding service jobs?

When workers left an industry to which they were attached, they moved into the industry in which they would be working at the end of the three-year follow-up period relatively quickly, within about a half a year. The gap between jobs was not necessarily spent unemployed; part of it was spent employed in some other industry or employed in multiple industries as the worker made the transition from one job to another.

In general, the attached workers who changed industries in Montana were *not* primarily leaving declining sectors of the economy. The rates at which workers left such contracting industries as forest products and metal mining and smelting were below the average rate for all industries; for expanding industries such as travel and trade, the departure rates were above average. In other words, it would have been impossible to predict reliably how workers were moving through the economy on the basis of changes in the aggregate structure of employment. This result is not as counterintuitive as it might seem. The rapidly expanding industries, trade and travel, provided large numbers of entry-level jobs for which pay was relatively low. On the other hand, contracting natural resource industries provided relatively well-paid jobs to which workers were likely to try to stay attached even as the industries contracted.

The growth rates of the different industries did appear to play a greater role in determining the industries to which previously attached workers moved. Although contracting industries continued to attract and hire some of these shifting workers, a larger share of shifting workers tended to move toward expanding industries than toward contracting industries.

Only about one-fifth of those leaving relatively highly paid jobs in the contracting forest products industry moved into such poorly paid industries as travel and retail trade. They were most likely to move into construction, followed by other manufacturing, transportation, government, and business services.

In the rapidly expanding travel and retail industries, only one-third to one-half of new jobs were taken by workers moving from other industries to which they had previously been attached. This pattern indicates that the primary source of additional workers in these expanding sectors was new entrants into the workforce[27] rather than displaced workers from contracting sectors.

In general, moving from one industry to another improved workers' earning prospects.[28] Previously attached workers who shifted to a new industry or who worked in more than one industry at the end of the transition period saw their wages rise significantly more than did attached workers who stayed put.[29] That is not to say that staying attached to a single industry was bad for workers: those who did so saw their wages rise relative to the average of all workers. But those workers who changed industries and remained employed did even better.

This clearly indicates that shifting employment from one industry to another is not usually bad for workers, even workers with some tenure in a particular industry. This fact and the earlier observation that workers often leave expanding industries suggest that most such job shifts are voluntary. They are a strategy workers employ to improve their relative position rather than an involuntary expulsion forced on them by declines in the industry in which they have been working.[30]

Although shifting workers on average saw their relative wages rise by 12 percent with respect to those of workers who did not change industries, that was not true of all types of industry shift.[31] Attached workers who left industries in which wages ranged from below average to modestly above average saw substantial improvements in relative wages compared with those who did not shift. For instance, the travel industry paid wages that were only about 60 percent of the average. Attached travel workers who moved to another industry saw their relative wages rise by almost one-third more than those workers who remained in travel. On the other hand, jobs in forest products and mining paid wages that were 56 percent and 118 percent, respectively, above average. Attached workers who left those sectors saw their relative wages decline by 12 percent and 9 percent, respectively, compared with workers who remained in those industries. Given the very high wage premiums these workers were earning in forest products and mining, the modest declines in relative wages on leaving suggest that these workers were able to find employment in other relatively highly paid industries.

How relative wages change as workers detach from particular industries partially explains the pattern of industrial shifts we observed earlier. Workers leaving travel, trade, and other services could, on average, expect to improve their relative wage substantially by moving from those industries. Workers in mining, forest products, and public utilities could not. It is not surprising, then, that the rate of detachment in the former group of industries is high and that in the latter group is low.

It is important to note that this characterization of the effects of job change focuses on the *average* experience of workers changing industries. How representative is the average? That depends in part on the distribution of outcomes—that is, whether the experiences of workers are quite similar or quite diverse. In a related analysis of workers who changed industries in Montana, we found that in fact the effects of a change in industry on relative wages showed a wide dispersion.[32] Some workers experienced large gains, whereas others experienced significant losses. In that analysis, workers changing industries saw their relative wages rise by 33 percent. The median worker, however, saw only an 8 percent increase. That suggests that for almost half of the workers changing industries, there was little or no increase or an actual decline in relative wages. The high average effect is explained by the large gains by a minority of workers, which offset the losses of other workers who changed industries. Similar disparities in the experiences of individuals were observed among workers shifting out of or into particular industries.

SO WHAT *DID* DRIVE WAGES DOWNWARD?

Thus far in this chapter, we have reached an important conclusion: it is not primarily the change in economic structure of the Mountain West that has caused average pay to decline. It is nonetheless true that average pay *has* declined. And if changes in the structure of employment were not the cause, the obvious question is, What was?

In part, the answer is that what happened in the Mountain West may simply have mirrored what was happening in the rest of the country. From the mid-1970s to the late 1990s, average real wages all across the country largely stagnated. And behind the average, the picture is bleaker: for almost 80 percent of the male workforce, real weekly wages declined between 1973 and 1994. It was only increases in the real wages of the better-paid one-half of the female workforce and the best-paid one-fifth of male workers that kept the overall average weekly wage from declining (Gottschalk 1997, pp. 26–27).

It is important to recognize that the experience of workers in the Mountain West was driven in the main by these developments in the national labor market. In the following sections, we explore the economic interactions between the national and local economies, emphasizing the fact that the relationship between the two is an asymmetric one in which national forces can influence the local economy but most local economies are too small to have a national effect. We then describe some of the national trends that have been affecting the Mountain West along with the rest of the country.

Closed and Open Economies

National and local economies are often discussed in the same terms, the implicit assumption being that scale aside, they operate in pretty much the same way. But, in fact, there are numerous and important differences between them. In the determination of wages, one crucial difference is the degree of openness to the larger supranational or national economies in which they are embedded.

In many important respects, the markets of national economies are closed. This is particularly true of the labor market, in part because most governments restrict the movement of workers and their families across national boundaries.

Almost all countries have policies limiting the in-migration of workers and new permanent residents, and these policies are reinforced by the barriers imposed by language, culture, family ties, and the other attachments that potential in-migrants have to their own countries.

In a national economy that can control the entry of workers from outside its boundaries, when the demand for workers with a particular set of qualifications increases, these workers' wages will tend to rise. Conversely, a decline in demand will tend to lower their wages. If higher wages draw a larger percentage of the population into the labor force, lead workers to work longer hours, or motivate workers who do not have the required qualifications to invest in getting them, the upward pressure on wages may be diminished. But that type of change in labor force participation, average workweek, and skills of the labor force takes place slowly as social patterns and lifestyles change. The important point is that when an economy is closed to workers from the outside, an increase in the demand for labor has a predictable tendency to raise wages.

Local economies are quite different. They clearly are not closed. There are no legal limits on the local movement of workers, goods, capital, and other economic activities. When, in 1789, the United States abandoned its original Articles of Confederation and adopted the United States Constitution, states and local areas surrendered the right to control the flow of people and economic activity across their borders. This constitutionally protected "openness" of American local economies laid the basis for the creation of an integrated national economy within which workers, capital, and goods are highly mobile. The openness of local economies in the United States is a fundamental economic fact that must be accounted for in any discussion of the local economy and public economic policy.

Within the national economy, capital flows at the speed of electronic funds transfers. Goods move at the high speeds supported by the interstate highway system, jet aircraft, overnight courier systems, and the inventory maintenance programs of national retail and wholesale companies. Labor, too, moves readily. Each year during the 1980s and 1990s, 6 percent of the U.S. population migrated across county lines, and 3 percent migrated across state lines. In the second half of the twentieth century, tens of millions of Americans moved from center cities to suburbs, from the industrialized Northeast and Midwest to the South and West, and, in the last quarter of the century, from metropolitan to non-metropolitan areas. Families and individuals were ready and willing to move considerable distances in pursuit of what they perceived to be more attractive economic opportunities or living environments. These free and massive flows of people, goods, and capital clearly distinguish local economies, with no economic borders, from national economies, with whatever economic borders their governments choose to impose.[33]

In open local economies, an increase in the demand for certain types of workers is not likely to lead to higher wages. Because workers are willing to move long distances to take up new jobs, it tends to be the national labor market that sets wage levels for different types of workers. If within a local economy a wage is set that is above the national level, workers will move in pursuit of those unusually high-paying jobs, and the increased labor supply will push the wage back down toward national levels. Similarly, if the wages offered locally are significantly below the national average, workers will tend to move out, pursuing wages closer to the national average at other locations. As a result, either local labor shortages will force wages upward or the business firm itself will have to shut down or leave the area in pursuit of an adequate labor supply.

The mobility of labor, of course, is not perfect, and this means that there is some play in the linkage between local and national labor markets. To some degree, wages can be affected by local labor market conditions. But to understand what happened to Mountain West workers in the 1980s and 1990s, why real wages declined for so many, we should look mainly to the sea changes that occurred in the national labor market during that period, not to local events.

One might hope the high local demand for workers and rising local wages would affect the national labor market, driving wages up nationally and thus making the higher local wage viable in the national market. But local economies are not large enough to have this type of effect on national labor markets, at least not in the United States. Local economies, especially non-metropolitan or small metropolitan economies, are likely to represent only a tiny sliver of the overall national economy. Total employment in the entire state of Montana in 1997, for instance, represented only 0.3 percent of total national employment. In only one industry, metal mining, did Montana provide significantly more than 1 percent of total national employment, and even in that industry Montana's employment was only 3.7 percent of the 1997 national total. For sub-state local economies outside the country's largest metropolitan areas, the relative importance of local economic activities to the national economy would be even smaller—tiny fractions of 1 percent. This means that although changes in the national economy can have a substantial effect on the local economy, the reverse is not true. Significant economic influences flow in only one direction: from the national to the local level.

In general, national labor markets and the mobility of workers, firms, resources, and goods will strongly influence the wage levels in any particular locale. Policy makers will be ineffective or worse if they craft local economic policies in the mistaken belief that wages are set largely locally and without reference to national labor market trends.

Changes in the National Wage Structure: Declining Wages for Less Educated Workers

Since the mid-1970s, there has been a dramatic change in the relative wages associated with education and experience. For workers with high levels of education and work experience, real wages have risen, whereas for those with low levels of education and experience, they have fallen. This is especially true for men, whose real wages have declined while women's have increased. Workers without a high school diploma saw their real wages fall by about 15 percent between 1978 and 1989 while college graduates saw an 11 percent increase (Murphy and Welch 1993, p. 113). This divergence in economic fortunes took place at a time when the percentage of the workforce with a college education was rising significantly and the percentage of high school dropouts was declining. If the wages of skilled, well-educated workers rose even as their numbers increased, the demand for such workers must have been expanding rapidly. On the other hand, if the wages of poorly skilled and educated workers fell even as they were becoming more scarce, the demand for these workers must have been falling.

Two explanations have been offered for this shift in labor demand. One assumes that technological change has been *skilled labor intensive,* possibly because of the introduction of computers and other advanced technology into the workplace. The other explanation focuses on the effect on the U.S. economy of expanded international trade. The hypothesis is that the globalization of the economy has led the United States to specialize in more skill-intensive, high-technology manufacturing and professional services while relying on imports for less skill-intensive manufactured goods. Lower-technology manufacturing has shifted overseas, reducing the demand for less skilled workers in the United States. At the same time, professional services and high-technology manufacturing in the United States have expanded dramatically, boosting the demand for more highly skilled workers. Note that these explanations focus not on shifts in employment between high-paying and low-paying *industries* but rather on the rising demand for more skilled workers and falling demand for less skilled workers, which has spread across all industries.

In the past, a significant number of poorly educated and unskilled workers could earn relatively high wages. Increasingly, that is no longer the case. The blue-collar path to a middle-class lifestyle has narrowed considerably. Workers without education, skill, or experience face very bleak job and earning prospects.

Workers in their late teens can no longer simply go to work for a unionized national corporation and earn relatively high wages for the rest of their working lives.

It is important to emphasize that this is a national trend; it is not confined to particular regions. The returns to less educated and less skilled workers have been falling across the country, in all regions. As pointed out earlier, wages for blue-collar workers have been falling in high-wage industries, too; often the declines in those industries have been even greater than in less well paid sectors. Heavy reliance on such premium sectors, although it may have raised average pay, did not protect workers and communities from declines in pay during the 1980s and 1990s.

Changes in Wage-Setting Institutions

All the downward pressure on the earnings of less educated workers cannot be explained by changes in the pattern of labor demand. Western European countries have faced the same technological developments and the same globalized economy, but the change in their wage structures has not followed the U.S. pattern (Fortin and Lemieux 1997, p. 76). This suggests that economic factors unique to the United States are also at work.

The wages associated with various types of economic activities are not determined only by the interaction of labor supply and labor demand. Unions, public policies, laws, traditions, and other wage-setting institutions play an important role. Minimum-wage laws, the strength of labor unions, limits on child labor and overtime work, economic regulation of certain sectors such as transportation and public utilities, unemployment and income support programs, limits on international immigration, and regulation of international trade are all examples of public policies that potentially can influence wage levels for various groups of workers.

During the late 1970s and early 1980s, two of these wage-setting institutions, the effective level of the minimum wage and the influence of labor unions, changed significantly. Expressed in 1997 dollars, the real value of the minimum wage declined from a high of $6.63 in 1978 to a low of $4.40 in 1989, a decrease of $2.23 per hour, or one-third of the 1978 real value. In 1981, the minimum wage equaled 43 percent of the average hourly earnings in manufacturing; by 1990, it was 31 percent. Over that period, the proportion of workers at or below the minimum wage fell from one in eight to one in twenty-five (Fortin and Lemieux 1997, p. 79). Clearly, the minimum wage became largely ineffective during the 1980s, though increases during the 1990s partially reversed this effect as the minimum wage regained $0.83 of the $2.23 loss incurred during the 1980s.

During the same period, 1979–1988, the rate of unionization in the United States declined precipitously. Among male workers, it declined by one-third, from 31 to 21 percent. Because of increased unionization among female government workers, the overall unionization rate among all workers declined somewhat less, from 24 to 17 percent (Fortin and Lemieux 1997, p. 80). At its peak in 1946, 35 percent of the workforce was unionized. During the 1990s, the rapid decline slowed and unionization rates stabilized somewhat.[34]

The fact that these two wage-setting institutions declined in influence during the 1980s, at the same time real pay declined for most workers and wage and income inequality dramatically increased, suggests that there might be a connection between these phenomena. Careful empirical analysis confirms that the changes in these labor market institutions did in fact play an important role in the deteriorating economic circumstances of many workers.

The fact that the average wage was rising while the economic fortunes of most workers, especially those with low skill levels, were deteriorating means that inequality in the distribution of wages was growing. As workers at the lower end of the wage distribution saw their real wages fall and workers at the upper end saw theirs rise, the overall dispersion of wages increased, as did the gap between the upper and lower ends of the wage distribution. The empirical evidence indicates that 30 to 50 percent of the increase in inequality during the 1980s can be attributed to the declines in the two labor market institutions just discussed, minimum wages and unionization (DiNardo, Fortin, and Lemieux 1996, p. 1031; Fortin and Lemieux 1997, p. 89).

The effects of these two institutions have not been the same on all workers. Although its effect on men was significant, the decline in the real value of the minimum wage particularly expanded wage inequality among women. It allowed the wages of more female workers to drift to the lowest level. Changes in the rate of unionization, on the other hand, had almost no effect on women but a significant effect on men. That effect was primarily on workers in the middle of the wage distribution, which "thinned out" as wages for more of these workers were pushed toward the lower end of the earnings distribution.

These changes in wage-setting institutions had a substantially greater effect on wage inequality than did the changing industrial structure of the economy. Although changes in wage-setting institutions can explain 20 to 50 percent of the increase in wage inequality, industrial shifts in employment can explain only 5 to 10 percent.

CONCLUSION

The shift in employment opportunities from goods-producing to non-goods-producing industries or away from natural resource industries is not the primary cause of the decline in pay per job that has characterized the Mountain West. Eighty-five to 95 percent of that decline would have taken place anyway, even if the structure of employment could have been frozen in the form it took in the late 1970s. Pay per job fell because of downward pressure on wages in *all* sectors, including the natural resource industries and other goods-producing industries. Often, pay per job fell more in the traditional high-wage goods-producing industries than it did in the often disparaged service, trade, and tourism industries. Any explanation for the decline in pay has to focus on the downward pressures that cut across industry lines and pervaded most of the national economy.

The behavior of average earnings does not necessarily accurately reveal what is happening to workers individually as their work careers unfold. During the 1990s, as the structure of Montana's economy continued to shift away from reliance on natural resource industries, most of the state's workers experienced considerable stability in employment. After entering the labor force, most of them quickly became attached to a particular industry and continued with that industry through the study period, which ended in 1996. The 14 percent who did not become attached to an industry fared far worse in terms of relative wages.

Of those who became attached to a particular industry, about 17 percent ultimately left that industry and ended the study period in another or more than one other industry. On average, those who shifted industry *improved* rather than damaged their relative position. Even those who left the most highly paid industries faced only modest declines in relative income. In general, they were able to protect their relatively high pay despite the industry shift. The pattern of industry shifts clearly indicates that most were undertaken voluntarily in order to improve relative wages; on average, workers succeeded in doing so. There is little sign of a large displacement of workers from high- to low-wage industries with an accompanying catastrophic drop in wages. It is important to note, however, that we could not track discouraged workers who left covered employment in Montana.[35]

Local economies differ from the national economy in their lack of any barrier to the influx and outflow of people seeking jobs. Although an increase in demand for certain types of labor in the national labor market will tend to exert upward pressure on wages, an increase in the demand for labor in the local labor market will primarily lead to the movement of more people into that area rather than to higher wages. Local wage levels will primarily be tied to trends in the national labor market.

There are national economic forces that explain at least part of the downward pressure on real pay in the Mountain West. There appear to have been important shifts in the demand for different types of labor, with demand for highly educated and skilled workers outstripping a rising supply and demand for less skilled workers falling faster than that shrinking supply. In addition, labor market institutions, in particular the effective minimum wage and the rate of unionization, that had been important in the past in supporting wage levels at the middle and lower end of the wage distribution were significantly weakened during the 1980s, when the real wages of most workers deteriorated.

National labor market trends may explain why real pay stagnated or declined in the Mountain West, but it is not clear that they can explain why pay there fell *relative* to the national average. Clearly, something was going on in the Mountain West that was particular to that region.

In the foregoing discussion of national wage trends and national labor markets, we assumed that only wage levels were of concern to workers and their families. We argued that in response to higher or lower local wages, people would move from lower- to higher-wage areas, thus tending to equalize across the country the pay for each type of labor. In making decisions about where they want to live, however, workers and their families are likely to be concerned about more than just the wages they can earn in one place or another. The cost of living (particularly the cost of housing), the quality of schools and other public services, the friendliness or familiarity of the area, crime risks, climate, cultural and recreational opportunities, levels of pollution and congestion, and the like may all be given some consideration. Just as the local cost of living determines the actual purchasing power of local pay, other local characteristics help determine the overall level of satisfaction a family can achieve locally given the level of pay there. Because workers and their families will be willing to sacrifice at least some income in pursuit of the local qualities most important to them, they will be willing to accept lower wages in some locations and will demand higher wages in others. As a result, local wages *can* deviate from national averages even though national labor markets play an important role in setting local wage levels. It is such local differences in real pay, tied to important local site characteristics, to which we turn in the next chapter.

NOTES

1. In other contexts, occupation is also important. Physicians, for example, are usually said to have better jobs than convenience store clerks. But we take for granted that when people speak of the need for good jobs in the local economy, they are not referring to the need to train clerks to be physicians or to bring in more physicians. Rather, they are referring to the need for jobs in industries that pay higher wages to workers with the clerks' qualifications.
2. This is not to say that in the competitive model, changes in industrial structure have no effect on wages; in fact, they can. See the appendix for more on this subject.
3. Similarly, some industries pay below-average wages for workers of equivalent characteristics. The wage premium is not necessarily positive.
4. Average pay may not actually rise. If these new jobs pay no more than existing basic jobs and if expenditures associated with the new jobs put other in-migrants to work in relatively low-paid jobs, average pay may not increase; it could even decrease.
5. Bound and Johnson were attempting to explain changes in the *structure* of wages— that is, how wages of various demographic groups had changed relative to one another. Over the period, this structure had changed markedly; in particular, relative to poorly educated workers, well-educated workers had made dramatic wage gains, women had moved up somewhat in comparison with men, and experienced men had gained relative to their less experienced counterparts. Structural change proved to have little to do with these developments.
6. This estimate of the average annual wage for men in 1978 is illustrative, as is the estimate for workers with less than a high school education that immediately follows. The annual wage was approximated using hourly wage data from Mishel, Bernstein, and Schmitt 1996, p. 146, table 3.9; p. 167, table 3.18.
7. Note that our analyses are intended to explain the behavior of *pay per job,* whereas most of the national-level studies cited previously concerned implicit *hourly wages*—that is, hourly wages computed by dividing reported annual earnings by reported annual hours of work. See chapter 2 for a discussion of the distinction between these two pay measures.
8. There is also a residual component associated with the interaction of changes in the structure of employment and changes in pay.
9. For this procedure to make sense, it is necessary to assume that changes in wages are substantially independent from changes in structure. But if an industry is expanding (or contracting) locally, should that not increase (or reduce) the wages it pays? We assume that over the relatively long periods examined here, wages are determined mainly in national labor markets, and variations in local demand for labor in various industries have a negligible effect on the national market. In effect, then, we assume that *by industry,* wages in the Mountain West would have moved much as they did whether or not the observed changes in industrial structure had occurred.
10. Freezing the structure of employment at some previous date does not freeze the level of employment at that past level. Rather, it freezes the percentage share of total

employment at a past level. This allows actual employment in each sector to grow proportionately as the overall economy expands.

11. As table 4.1 shows, changes in the industrial structure of employment did push earnings per job down slightly. Over the 1978–1988 period, when earnings fell a long way, the depressing effect of changing industrial structure was relatively unimportant; other factors drove almost all the decline. Over the longer period, 1978–1998, there was not much decline to account for—3.4 percent—and as a result, the modest effect of structural change became more important.

12. Since there are unequal numbers of jobs in the two sectors of the economy, the fall in pay per job for all jobs is a *weighted* average of the fall in pay per job in each sector. The weight for each sector is its percentage of all jobs. Thus, in this example the decline in average pay for all jobs is $2,572, which equals $(0.08) \times (\$5,513) + (0.92)(\$2,316)$.

13. Some might argue that if there had been such a boom in employment in these higher-wage sectors, wages would not have been depressed in those sectors and average pay would not have declined as much. As discussed in footnote 9 in this chapter, wage levels in a local economy are largely influenced by national economic forces. The workforce is highly mobile and firms are unlikely to have difficulty attracting the workforce they need, especially in high-amenity areas. This is especially true for higher-wage firms. After all, the overall rapid expansion of employment in the Mountain West did not lead to higher wages. To the contrary, real wages fell as employment expanded significantly.

14. In the first decomposition in table 4.2, goods production is reported in non-farm terms because agricultural earnings per job fell from $25,000 to $4,000 during the period as a result of drought and low farm prices. The year 1978 was a relatively good one for agriculture, whereas 1988 was a relatively poor one. In order to avoid skewed results due to these cyclical fluctuations in farm incomes, the farm sector was removed. If it had been left in the calculation, the effect of changes in industrial structure would have been even smaller.

15. Recall that services include professional, personal, and repair services but exclude a variety of non-goods-producing activities such as trade, finance, and government.

16. For the present purposes, we define a high-wage industry as one in which pay per job is one-third or more above the average for all industries.

17. A table similar to tables 4.1 and 4.2 but providing pay per job and employment share information on all seventy industries included in this analysis is available from the authors on request.

18. Timber dependency was defined as 10 percent or more of county earnings originating in the lumber sector in 1990. Those counties were identified by the USDA Forest Service (McGinnis, Schuster, and Stewart 1996).

19. The division of the economy used in the analysis of timber-dependent counties of the Pacific Northwest was between goods production, of which timber harvest and processing was an important part, and the non-goods-producing sector. The analysis

of the southwestern Oregon counties focused specifically on the manufacturing sector, which consisted almost entirely of the lumber industry.

20. The statistical relationship between pay and its determinants is known as an earnings function; this concept is described in more detail in the appendix. For a complete discussion of this analysis, see Barrett 1999. The procedure for estimating the wage loss associated with its various causes follows Oaxaca 1973.

21. The statistics reported in this section are based on calculations by the authors using unpublished data provided by the Unemployment Insurance Division of the Montana Department of Labor and Industry. These data and the calculations are described in detail in Barrett 1998a and Barrett and Power 1997.

22. This is not to say that a decline in the average wage, even if it occurs as the wages of every individual in the group are rising, is always benign. If new members of the group are being placed on ever lower, albeit rising, wage trajectories, the group clearly is becoming slowly worse off. See the appendix for a more complete explanation of this point.

23. There is no Standard Industrial Classification (SIC) industry called "travel" or "tourism." For the analysis reported in this section, we created such an industry by aggregating the SIC industries (SIC code is indicated in parentheses) air transportation (45), gas stations (554), eating and drinking places (58), hotels and other lodging places (70), and automobile services (55). These industries absorb almost all tourist spending. For a complete explanation of the industry classifications used in this study, see Barrett and Power 1997, p. 28.

24. The Census Bureau, in its Current Population Survey, tracks a sample of people it interviews over a two-year period, but the workers are not uniquely identified, and this is not a sufficient time period to see how workers moving between jobs are affected.

25. State unemployment insurance programs cover the vast majority of workers. The most significant minority not covered by this data is the self-employed, who in Montana represent 10 to 15 percent of all workers. Because many of the second jobs of multiple job holders involve self-employment, self-employment jobs represent a much larger share—25 percent—of total jobs in Montana.

26. These 250,000 histories make up approximately 80 percent of the 318,588 wage histories at our disposal that included at least two years of employment. Twenty percent were excluded either because information about the industry of employment was missing for one or more quarters (this results when employers fail to file on time) or because the two-year employment period ended after the beginning of 1994.

27. New entrants into the Montana labor force include residents who begin to work or existing workers who move to Montana from other states. In addition, since we are considering the *covered* labor force, a small number of new entrants are residents who were working previously but who were self-employed or otherwise not covered by state unemployment insurance.

28. It is important to recognize that in this discussion, the change in wages experienced by

any group of Montana workers is assessed relative to the change experienced by other such groups or the Montana labor force at large. That a group—say, job changers— did well relative to another group (non-changers) does not mean that the group's real wages were rising or that it was doing well compared with workers elsewhere in the country.

29. Employment in the three-year follow-up period could be in any industry and was not necessarily continuous.

30. This positive conclusion about the group of workers we tracked has to be tempered by the fact that we could not track workers who left the state, left covered employment, retired, or became discouraged and left the workforce completely. The outcomes for that group of "job shifters" may well have been much less positive.

31. In this and the following results, the calculated relative wage after the industry shift ignores any period of unemployment in the transition and reflects the relative wage only for the quarters during which the worker was actually working.

32. See Barrett and Power 1997. That analysis focused on workers who spent at least two years in one industry and then made a transition to another industry in which they also worked for at least two years. That sample of workers was only half as large as the one reported on earlier.

33. The national government's ability to impose economic borders can to some degree be attenuated by illegal immigration, smuggling, and the like.

34. The manufacturing sector of the national economy was the most unionized. As the relative importance of manufacturing declined, that structural change by itself would have tended to reduce the degree of unionization. Unionization in manufacturing, however, declined dramatically on its own as manufacturing shifted from the Northeast to the South and West, where "right to work" laws created a less hospitable climate for union organizing. In addition, even in the Northeast, non-union plants became socially and politically more acceptable. In short, there was an important institutional change rather than just a change in industrial structure.

35. As noted before, 16 percent of workers who became attached to an industry left covered employment within three years. Because they cannot be tracked, we do not know how many of these workers stopped working altogether, became self-employed, or left Montana. It is reasonable to assume that in some of these cases, workers left covered employment because they had been forced out of one job and were unable to make a successful transition to another, but it is impossible to assess how frequently this happened.

CHAPTER 5

~~≋≋~~ Is the Mountain West Really Poor?

Size of Place and Relative Pay and Income

I f workers in the Mountain West saw their real wages stagnate over the last two decades of the twentieth century, they could take some comfort in the fact that at least they were not alone; rather, they were part of a national trend. As we saw in the preceding chapter, the decline in natural resource employment that marked the region's changing economic structure appears to have had little to do with the overall fall in wages in the region during that period. In other words, wages did not fall because workers were moving from high-paying natural resource employment to low-paying service jobs. Rather, most of the decline occurred because wages were falling in *all* industries, echoing what was happening to workers in *every* part of the country. Following the recession of 1982, the U.S. economy experienced an almost uninterrupted period of economic growth; in the 1990s in particular, growth was sustained and dramatic. But the troubling fact remained that despite all this apparent success, real wages in the United States grew very slowly on average, and for a significant part of the workforce, they fell. Workers in the Mountain West could not escape this trend, of course, but they were not its only victims.

That wage developments in the Mountain West tracked those in the rest of the country does not, however, tell the whole story. The fact is that in the early 1970s, just before real wage growth sputtered to a near halt all across the country, pay per job in the Mountain West was already 5 percent below the national average. And when wages did begin to decline, they did so more sharply in the Mountain West than elsewhere, so that by 1998 pay per job was 11 percent below the national average in the region as a whole and 33 percent below the national average in Montana. In pay per job, five of the eight Mountain West states (Montana, Wyoming, Idaho, New Mexico, and Utah) ranked among the lowest fifteen states in the country, with Montana dead last in both the region and the country.

Needless to say, these rankings hurt. They were seen as evidence that residents of the Mountain West were not living as well as other Americans, that poverty was regionally endemic, and that there was something especially wrong with the way the regional economy was working. There were plenty of potential culprits on which the crisis could be blamed, including high taxes, poor business climate, restrictive federal environmental and resource policies, and cutthroat foreign competition. And for every culprit there was a solution, which typically involved de-funding of government, dismantling of established environmental protections, exhaustive exploitation of publicly owned resources, or some other risky gambit aimed at "attracting good, high-paying jobs."

Although the Mountain West's deep economic distress seemed unquestionable and appeared to justify desperate measures, the region failed to display one of the classic symptoms of a region in trouble: an exodus of workers seeking better opportunities elsewhere. Americans are, in fact, highly mobile, and historical examples of their willingness to pull up stakes and move on are abundant: young people left the country's hard-pressed farms for jobs in urban areas, African Americans abandoned the impoverished and segregated rural South for the promise of northern cities, middle-class families moved from troubled central cities to suburbs, and industrial workers fled the decaying Rust Belt of the Northeast for the Sun Belt of the Southwest. But in the Mountain West in the 1980s and 1990s, as incomes and wages fell relative to those in the rest of the country, none of that happened. Indeed, rather than moving out of the region, people moved in; the relationship between wages and migration was turned on its head.

As odd as this pattern of movement may seem, it was not confined to the Mountain West. As illustrated in figure 5.1, during the 1990s Americans in general tended to move into states where average personal income was low and out of states where it was high; there is little evidence that people were moving to avoid economic distress. Note in figure 5.1 that six of the eight Mountain West states fall into the category of having net in-migration despite having below-average incomes. We turn in this chapter to an explanation of this seemingly strange behavior and its implications for understanding economic well-being in the Mountain West.

We conclude that although pay and income are lower in the Mountain West than in the rest of the country, the shortfall is offset by important attractions available to residents: lower living costs and the amenities of small-city and

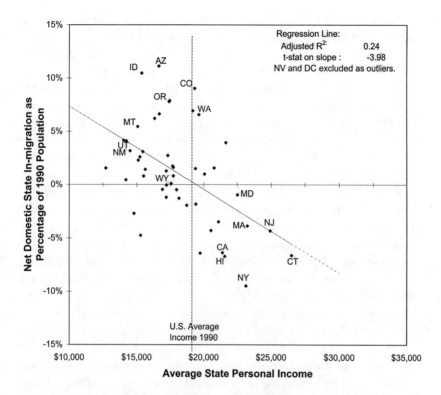

FIGURE 5.1. Per capita incomes and rates of net in-migration for U.S. states, 1990–1997. The regression line shows a statistically estimated inverse relationship between 1990 state per capita income and the rate of net state in-migration for 1990–1997. People moved out of high-income states and into low-income states. *Source:* Prepared by the authors using data from Bureau of Economic Analysis 1999 and U.S. Census Bureau 2000a.

rural living, scenic beauty, and opportunities for outstanding outdoor recreation. All these are public goods that provide residents with the equivalent of a "second paycheck" that compensates for lower pay and income. Because of this compensation, the economic well-being of people in the region matches that of other Americans, even if their dollar income is less.

REGIONAL DIFFERENCES IN WAGES: SOME BASIC THEORY

Wages and earnings throughout the United States vary substantially by state and region. For example, the Census Bureau reported that in 1997 median annual family income for the country as a whole was $37,005. But by state, this figure ranged from a high of $48,021 in New Jersey to a low of $26,162 in Arkansas (U.S. Census Bureau 1999b, table 748). Of course, these states differ in ways that can explain part of this large gap: a significantly larger part of the population was employed in New Jersey than in Arkansas—64.3 percent, compared with 59.8 percent. In addition, all of New Jersey's residents lived in metropolitan areas, most in the greater New York metropolitan area, with its 20 million inhabitants. As a result, they were likely to face much higher living costs than were residents of Arkansas, only 48.3 percent of whom lived in two metropolitan areas of well fewer than 700,000 inhabitants each.[1] It is also possible that the income gap observed in any one year is atypical and would shrink over a longer period of time. But the fact remains that even when we take into account differences between state economies and consider long periods of time, interstate and inter-regional differences in earnings and income are large and persistent.

In understanding these differences, the first step is to recognize that each region (and within regions, each locality) has a unique set of conditions that affect both the attractiveness of living and the cost of doing business in that place. On the attractiveness side, we can include such features as climate, school quality, personal security, cultural and recreational opportunities, and the health of the social and natural environments. Where costs are concerned, things that make living in a place attractive to individuals and families also implicitly reduce business costs, because workers as well as business owners are willing to accept lower incomes in order to enjoy local amenities. Other features of a locality may affect business costs explicitly: proximity to markets, public infrastructure such as roads and communications facilities, research and development capabilities, tax rates, and so forth.

Differences in these conditions from one place to another give rise to differences in incomes, through a process in which migration is the driving force. Suppose, for example, that workers in two localities—say, Los Angeles and Boise, Idaho—earned the same wages and faced the same housing costs.[2] Suppose further that workers considered the quality of life to be better in Boise than in Los Angeles. In that case, they would move to Boise, where, as a result, there would be a tendency for wages to fall and housing costs to rise. Eventually, wages would fall, housing costs would rise, or both, enough to choke off migration; the two cities would reach an equilibrium in which permanent differentials in wages and housing costs would prevail, reflecting differences in local quality of life. Such differences are said to be *compensating*—that is, in this case, workers in Los Angeles are compensated with higher wages or lower rents for living in a city with inferior quality of life.

It is an important feature of compensating differentials that they do *not* reflect differences in economic well-being. In our example, the higher wages received by workers in Los Angeles compensate them for the inferior quality of life in that city, but we could just as well say that the superior quality of life in Boise compensates workers there for their lower wages and higher rents. Although their earnings differ, workers in the two cities are equally well off. In Los Angeles, they enjoy more income and fewer amenities; in Boise, less income but more amenities. The point is that people move to where the value of the whole package—wages, housing, and local amenities—is higher. Where people move in, the value of the package starts out high but falls; in the places they leave, it starts out low but rises. Eventually it is a wash, and people stop moving.

Consider now the effect of local differences in the cost of doing business. We can return to the case of Los Angeles and Boise, again imagining that we start in a situation in which wages and housing costs are the same in the two cities. Suppose, moreover, that because of its small size and remote location, Boise is an expensive place for firms to operate, at least when compared with Los Angeles. In this situation, firms will move to Los Angeles and compete for labor and space, driving up wages and rents; in Boise, wages and rents will fall.[3] Eventually, business costs in the two cities will be about the same, removing the incentive for firms to migrate to one city or the other.

Quality-of-life and business cost effects can combine in a way that makes it hard to predict how wages and rents will vary between any two locations. Suppose, for example, that Los Angeles were both a cheap place to do business (which would attract firms) and an unpleasant place to live (which would repel workers).[4] Then wages would certainly be higher there, but it would be impossible to predict just how rents might behave. On the other hand, imagine a town with low business costs and outstanding living amenities. Both firms and workers would be attracted to such a place, with an unpredictable effect on wages but an almost certain rise in rents as workers seek housing and firms seek space in which to do business. The important result remains, however, that migration of firms and workers tends to produce a spatial pattern of wages and rents that equalizes both economic well-being and the cost of doing business between any two localities.[5]

Although we find this type of theorizing somewhat persuasive, we do not think it is safe to dismiss the problem of low wages in the Mountain West by simply assuming that quality of life compensates workers in the region for lower earnings. For one thing, we want to avoid the circular reasoning involved in concluding that (a) workers earn less because of the high quality of life and (b) the quality of life must be high because workers earn less. We think it is important to find *independent* evidence of quality-of-life differences.

Another reason to be wary has to do with migration. In this theory, geographic wage and rent differentials are fully compensated for by quality-of-life differences only when net migration is zero (or at least quite low). Suppose this condition is not met and we observe a low-wage area that people are leaving. We have to conclude that people think they will be better off somewhere else and that quality of life in the area does not completely make up for wages being low. Of course, as figure 5.1 demonstrates, the opposite is also possible: people can and do move to low-wage areas and evidently think they will be better off for doing so even if their wages fall as a result.

Thus, we cannot simply assume that low wages in the Mountain West are a reflection, or, for that matter, a measure, of high quality of life. We need some other evidence that this is the case. In the following sections, we provide some details about the region's wage shortfall and about the pattern of in- and out-migration that we think provides that evidence.

EARNINGS AND COMMUNITY SIZE

Across the United States, community size is an important influence on what workers earn; in general, the bigger a town or city is, the better its residents are paid. This is confirmed in figure 5.2, which shows the relationship between average earnings per job and population for the 315 standard metropolitan areas in the United States.[6] Note that several of the Mountain West's small metropolitan areas were among those with the lowest pay and smallest populations in the country.

When it comes to comparing average earnings in the Mountain West and the rest of the country, the relationship between community size and earnings becomes critical. Because most residents of the Mountain West live in relatively small cities or rural areas, whereas most other Americans live in large metropolitan areas, in comparing regional and national averages we are dealing with apples and oranges. Although half of all Americans live in thirty-two cities with 1997 populations in excess of 1.4 million, only 31 percent of the Mountain West's population lives in cities that large; although almost 40 percent of the country's population lives in cities of 3 million or more, the region has no cities of that size. Average earnings for the Mountain West are dragged down by the preponderance within the region of small cities, but for the rest of the country it is the other way around. Average earnings for the country therefore exceed those of the region at least in part because in using averages, we are comparing the small cities and rural areas of the Mountain West with huge metropolitan areas elsewhere.

To avoid this problem, we should compare the region's non-metropolitan areas only with non-metropolitan areas in the rest of the country and the region's

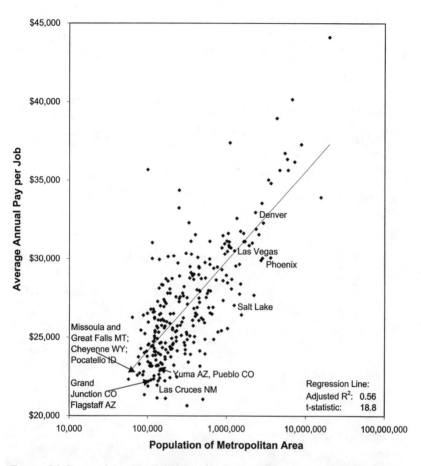

FIGURE 5.2. Pay per job and populations of U.S. metropolitan areas, 1997. The regression line shows a statistically estimated positive relationship between the size of a metropolitan area and pay per job; population size is measured on a logarithmic scale. A tenfold increase in the size of a metropolitan area is associated with an increase in pay per job of about $5,000. *Source:* Prepared by the authors using data from Bureau of Economic Analysis 1999.

cities only with cities of similar size across the country. This is done in figure 5.3, which shows that when we control for community size in this way, differences in earnings between the Mountain West and the rest of the country largely disappear; only for the early 1980s, when earnings in non-metropolitan areas were about 10 percent *higher* in the Mountain West than in the rest of the country, is any gap between the region and the country noticeable.[7] In other words, the gap between nationwide and region-wide earnings per job is almost entirely due to the fact that most westerners live in smaller communities than other Americans do.[8]

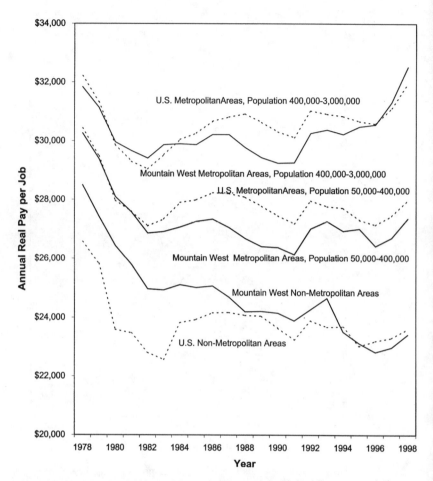

FIGURE 5.3. Real pay per job in the Mountain West and the United States as a whole by size of place, 1978–1998 (1998 dollars). For places of equivalent size, there was little difference between the region and the country as a whole in either levels or trends in real pay per job. *Source:* Bureau of Economic Analysis 1999.

Of course, knowing that low earnings in the region are really due to the fact that residents live in smaller cities and rural areas does not by itself make the problem of low earnings disappear. Only if we believe that small cities and rural areas are better places to live than big cities—with lower housing costs, healthier and safer environments, more supportive and richer social institutions, less pressured lifestyles, and the like—can we conclude that lower earnings are not much to worry about. Stated otherwise, if the high wages of big-city residents are simply compensation for astronomical rents and the provocations of life in the megalopolis, Americans living in small cities in the Mountain West, or anywhere else, for that matter, may have lower incomes than their big-city compatriots, but their standard of living, all things considered, is about the same.

EXPLANATIONS FOR LOWER PAY IN SMALLER CITIES: COST OF LIVING

Measures that compare cost of living across geographic areas of the United States are hard to come by. For the country as a whole, cost of living is usually measured by the Consumer Price Index (CPI). In developing the CPI, the federal government does collect information about how the cost of living changes *over time* in the country's largest urban areas, but unfortunately these data do not tell us how the cost of living varies from one location to another. Such information was collected on a limited basis until the early 1980s, when the federal government got out of the geographic cost-of-living business. Since then, some private business organizations and economic researchers have tried to measure geographic differences in cost of living.

One such private sector estimate that is widely used is the ACCRA Cost of Living Index, published by ACCRA, a research organization supported by local chambers of commerce, federal- and state-level economic development offices, and community development professionals. This index is based on the prices of a large collection of items that ACCRA deems representative of the spending patterns of middle management employees. The value of the index—for example, 93.0 for Huntsville, Alabama, in the first quarter of 1998—gives the cost of selected items in a city as a percentage of the average cost of the same items across all metropolitan areas on which ACCRA reports (ACCRA 1998). Data are reported quarterly.

For this analysis, we calculated the 1998 annual average value of the quarterly cost-of-living index for 211 metropolitan areas (for areas that failed to report in every quarter, we used the average for reported quarters). ACCRA reports the index (1) for an entire metropolitan area, (2) for the central city alone, or (3) for the central city and other places within the metropolitan area. In the last case, we used the index reported for the central city.[9] We matched each city's cost-of-living data with figures from the Regional Economic Information System (REIS) for population and earnings per job.

To depict the relationship between earnings, cost of living, and city size, we calculated correlation coefficients, which are measures of the extent to which

Table 5.1. Cost of Living, Pay per Job, and Deflated Pay per Job by U.S. Metropolitan Area Population Size Class, 1998

Size of Population (× 1,000)	Cost of Living	Pay per Job	Deflated Pay per Job
> 2,000	128.0	$36,536	$28,544
1,000–2,000	100.5	$30,659	$30,507
500–1,000	98.9	$28,206	$28,520
250–500	100.0	$26,987	$26,987
< 500	97.7	$25,436	$26,035

Source: Computed by the authors using data from Bureau of Economic Analysis 1999 and ACCRA 1998.

variables are related to one another. These statistics show that cost of living is positively related to earnings, as are both earnings and cost of living to size of place.[10] The variation in cost of living and earnings with size of place is represented in another way in table 5.1, which shows average earnings and cost of living across cities in various size classes for 1998. In calculating these averages, we weighted values for each city by the share of the city's population in the total population for all reporting cities in the size class.

As expected, average earnings per job rose as size of place increased; cost of living rose over the entire range of size classes, although it took a small dip in moving from cities with populations of fewer than 500,000 to cities with populations of 500,000 to 1 million. Earnings per job in cities of more than 2 million were 43.6 percent higher than earnings per job in small cities of fewer than 500,000, but this difference is reduced to 9.6 percent when earnings are deflated by the local cost of living ([Earnings per job]/[Cost of living]). That is, almost 80 percent of the apparent gap in economic well-being is eliminated when cost-of-living differences are accounted for.

Subject to a number of caveats regarding the quality of ACCRA's cost-of-living data and the extent to which the sample can be considered representative (cities are included when local chambers of commerce choose to cooperate with ACCRA and submit price reports), the results reported in table 5.1 suggest that interurban variations in earnings per job largely compensate for differences in out-of-pocket cost of living. Corrected for differences in cost of living, interurban differentials in earnings are substantially reduced and the earnings advantage of living in a large metropolitan area almost disappears.

EXPLANATIONS FOR LOWER PAY IN SMALLER CITIES: QUALITY OF LIFE

Economists and real estate professionals devoted considerable research effort in the last half of the twentieth century to estimating the value people place on various characteristics of the local residential environment. As real estate agents say, location is everything. Each residential location provides a bundle of different qualities associated with its physical and social environment. Without conducting any formal economic analysis, most people are aware of the fact that property in high-crime, heavily polluted, noisy, congested, or run-down areas commands a lower price or rental value. On the other hand, property that provides access to better schools, libraries, and parks, that presents lower risks to person and property from crime, or that is located in more aesthetically pleasing neighborhoods commands much higher values.

People are willing to pay tens or hundreds of thousands of dollars to gain access to more attractive living environments. Clearly, people care about where they live, and they act economically in the pursuit of their preferences. The quality of living environments is by no means a trivial component of overall well-being. Because people are willing to make major economic sacrifices in pursuit of higher-quality environments, local environmental quality is an important consideration in assessing the economy's performance.

By assessing statistically the relationship between prices paid for homes in different locations and measures of the various environmental features characteristic of those locations, economists have been able to estimate what people are willing to pay to gain access to particular public amenities or to avoid the particular disadvantages of certain neighborhoods.[11] However, as discussed earlier, paying higher housing prices is just one way in which residents gain access to attractive mixes of public amenities. The other "entry fee" may be acceptance of lower wages and more limited economic opportunities resulting from the excess supply of workers who also want to enjoy those amenities.

Using data from the 1980 census, Glenn Blomquist, Mark Berger, and John Hoehn (1988) measured the values Americans placed on sixteen different amenities that varied from one location to another. They did this by observing what people were willing to pay, in higher rents, lower wages, or both, in order to have access to such amenities, which were represented by variables that measured proximity to a coast, crime rate, school quality, and several different dimensions of both climate and environmental quality. They then used these measures of willingness to pay to compute a quality-of-life index (QOLI), that is, the total value

Table 5.2. Average Quality-of-Life Index (QOLI) for
Counties by Population Size Class of Metropolitan
Areas in Which Counties Are Located, 1980

Size of Metropolitan Area (× 1,000)	Weighted Average QOLI
> 2,000	–$194
1,000–2,000	$257
500–1,000	$258
250–500	$316
< 250	$393

Source: Computed by the authors from estimates of QOLIs
for 253 counties in Blomquest, Berger, and Hoehn 1988
and from U.S. Census Bureau 1983, table B.

of the package of sixteen amenities that was available in each of 253 metropoli-
tan-area counties. The winner in this calculation was Pueblo County, Colorado;
the authors calculated that an average American family would put a value of
almost $6,600 (in 1999 dollars) on the mix of amenities available there. The loser
was St. Louis, Missouri, where the value of the package was so low that it actually would impose a cost of $3,700 on an average family. The difference between
these two is more than $10,000 per year in 1999 dollars. In both 1980 and 1997,
this difference, adjusted for inflation, represented 28 percent of the national median
household income—not a small economic matter.

The authors did not analyze how the counties' QOLIs varied with the sizes
of the metropolitan areas in which they were located, but that is not hard to do. In
table 5.2, we have placed each of the 253 counties in one of five groups, based on
the 1980 size of the metropolitan areas in which they are located, and calculated
the population weighted average QOLI for each group. Clearly, as the size of the
metropolitan area increased, the average QOLI fell. In moving from the smallest
to the largest group of cities, the value of the package of local amenities fell by
almost $600 in 1980 dollars, or $1,200 in 1999 dollars. As a measure of relative
magnitude, that $600 per year represented about 20 percent of the difference in
average pay per job between the groups of smaller and larger metropolitan areas.[12]

AMENITIES, COST OF LIVING, AND MIGRATION

One reason not to simply assume that the differences in earnings associated
with size of place compensate for differences in quality of life is that there is a
good deal of migration going on between places. This suggests that there are

still economic reasons to move between regions. For example, if workers are earning less in rural areas and also *leaving* those areas in large numbers, they are indicating that whatever the benefits of rural residence may be, they are not enough to compensate for lower earnings.

Is it possible to come up with a measure of how much less people would be willing to earn in order to live in one place rather than another, one that takes account of migration? Using data for the period 1971–1988, Michael Greenwood and colleagues (1991) did so by analyzing the relationship between interstate migration and state earnings (measured relative to the national average). On the basis of this analysis, they were able to estimate *equilibrium* relative earnings for each state, that is, the earnings at which net migration would stop. They judged differences in these equilibrium relative earnings to be correct measures of the value of the bundles of amenities available in the states. Their results suggest that the country's amenity-rich states are concentrated in the South and West. Interestingly, in many pairs of states, the difference in equilibrium earnings is larger than the difference in actual earnings. In these cases, the gaps in actual earnings tend to understate somewhat the true state-to-state differences in the value of local amenities.[13]

Figure 5.4 depicts the relationship between the equilibrium earnings for each state calculated by Greenwood and colleagues and the share of the state's population living outside of metropolitan areas. As expected, the less metropolitan a state, the lower the earnings that will attract *and hold* its population.[14] In other words, residents of the country's small cities, towns, and rural areas appear to accept lower earnings voluntarily as the price they pay to enjoy the special amenities available to them. The results shown in figure 5.4 indicate that earnings in most Mountain West states could be 20 to 30 percent below those in New Jersey, Connecticut, Maryland, and New York and not trigger out-migration from the Mountain West and in-migration to the higher-wage states. Of course, actual migration patterns confirm this: the relatively low-wage Mountain West states have in fact been gaining population from net in-migration while the high-wage states of the East Coast have been losing population to out-migration.

WHO PAYS THE PENALTY FOR LIVING IN THE MOUNTAIN WEST?

We have just seen that the size of the "penalty" paid for living in the Mountain West depends heavily on the size of communities where earnings are measured. It turns out that the penalty also varies quite a bit among individuals and that this

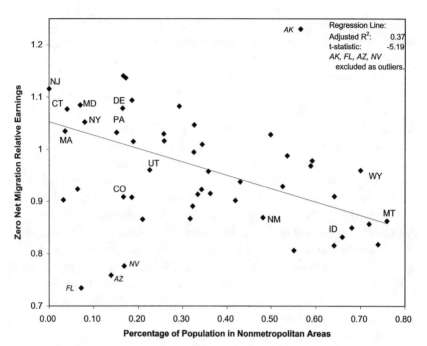

FIGURE 5.4. Zero net migration relative earnings and percentages of population in non-metropolitan areas of U.S. states, 1980. The regression line shows a statistically estimated negative relationship between the relative earnings level that would trigger zero net migration in a state and the percentage of the population in non-metropolitan areas. *Source:* Prepared by the authors using data from Bureau of Economic Analysis 1999 and zero net migration relative earnings estimates in Greenwood et al. 1991.

variation is related to the individuals' characteristics in interesting and revealing ways. In this section, we analyze some of those relationships and their implications in Montana, the Mountain West state where annual earnings are lowest.

Our analysis relies on *earnings functions,* which are equations that depict the numerical relationship between individual characteristics and earnings (see the appendix for a fuller description of earnings functions). The measure of earnings in this analysis is hourly wages, and the characteristics included in the earnings functions are age, education, race, marital status, occupation, and industry of employment. There are obviously other things—talent, attitude, and physical health, for example—that influence what a person earns, and we would like to take them into account. But the data available to describe groups of workers rarely contain measures of those traits.[15]

Table 5.3. Predicted Hourly Wages in the Montana and U.S. Labor Markets and the Montana Penalty, by Educational Attainment Alone and by Educational Attainment, Occupation, and Industry, 1990–1996

	Estimated Hourly Wage		
Educational Attainment	Montana	U.S.	Montana Penalty
	Educational Attainment Alone		
Less than high school	$7.04	$7.08	0.5%
High school	$8.06	$8.86	9.1%
Some college	$8.08	$9.69	16.7%
College graduate	$10.10	$11.75	14.1%
Post-graduate	$11.25	$13.74	18.1%
	Educational Attainment, Occupation, and Industry		
Less than high school	$5.81	$5.78	0.4%
High school	$7.98	$8.66	7.9%
Some college	$8.05	$9.68	16.8%
College graduate	$11.34	$13.45	15.7%
Post-graduate	$13.32	$16.69	20.2%

Source: Barrett 1998b.

Our procedure was to estimate two earnings functions, one for Montana and the other for the rest of the United States, excluding Montana. We then used these two functions to estimate what a worker with a particular set of characteristics would earn in Montana and in the rest of the country. The difference between these two figures is, in turn, our estimate of the penalty a worker with those characteristics pays for living and working in Montana rather than somewhere else. How these penalties vary with educational attainment and wage level are of particular interest.

In table 5.3, the section titled "Educational Attainment Alone" shows, for the period 1990–1996, how the penalty for living in Montana varied with educational attainment, measured by years of school completed. In estimating the wages used to calculate these penalties, in every case we considered workers with a uniform set of characteristics (except, of course, years of education) typical of the entire Montana labor force.[16] Obviously, as educational attainment increased, so did wages in both Montana and the rest of the country. But the rewards for additional education increased faster outside of Montana, and so more highly educated workers paid a higher penalty for living in the state than did less educated ones. For workers with less than a high school education, the penalty was essentially zero, and for those with post-graduate education (this would include professionals such as physicians, lawyers, and those with M.B.A. degrees and other advanced training), the penalty topped out at about 18 percent.

It might be objected that workers with different levels of education are not likely to be alike in all other respects, and this is what these calculations assume. In particular, educational level is likely to affect both the industry and the occupation an individual chooses. To account for this problem, the section of table 5.3 titled "Educational Attainment, Occupation, and Industry" shows estimated wages and the Montana penalty at different educational levels. In this case, however, wages at each level of education are estimated for workers in the occupations and industries of employment typical of Montana workers at that level. All other characteristics used in the estimates (gender, age, etc.) are uniform and typical of the Montana labor force. This change means that bigger wage increases are associated with higher educational level, a reflection of the fact that better-educated workers tend to go into higher-paying occupations and industries. The effect of educational attainment on the penalty for living in Montana becomes more pronounced as well. The penalty for workers with post-graduate education rises to a little more than 20 percent, and high school dropouts actually earn very slightly *more* in Montana than they would elsewhere (although, at less than $6 per hour, arguably still not enough to live on).

Table 5.4 shows how the penalty for living in Montana varied with the hourly wage level in 1990–1996. For each quintile of the hourly wage distribution, we have estimated, for both Montana and the rest of the country, the hourly wage of a worker with the average characteristics of the Montanans who actually occupy that quintile. Just as it does with rising education, the penalty workers pay for living in Montana generally goes up with increasing wages. Despite being well paid among Montanans, high-wage Montana workers are further behind their national counterparts than low-wage workers are; those in the middle of the distribution are the furthest behind.

The conclusion we draw from this evidence is this: the people who pay the highest penalty for living in Montana would be well equipped, with both education and income, to move to "better" opportunities outside the state if that were what they wanted to do. The fact that they do not means that they have consciously chosen to trade higher wages for the quality of life they can enjoy in the state. Their wages are high enough to provide them with the income they need, and they enjoy a rich mix of public amenities.

On the other hand, workers whose characteristics might most predispose them to being trapped in Montana and locked into inferior work opportunities in

Table 5.4. Predicted Hourly Wages in the Montana and
U.S. Labor Markets and the Montana Penalty, by
Hourly Wage Quintile, 1990–1996

Quintile	Predicted Hourly Wage		Montana Penalty
	Montana	U.S.	
First (lowest)	$ 5.79	$ 6.39	9.4%
Second	$ 7.02	$ 7.96	11.9%
Third (middle)	$ 8.38	$ 9.70	13.6%
Fourth	$10.40	$11.91	12.7%
Fifth (highest)	$12.12	$13.67	11.4%

Source: Barrett 1998b.

fact pay the lowest penalties or, indeed, no penalty at all for working in the state.

Many Montanans would find these conclusions hard to believe. After all, would most of them not like to take home the same pay as Californians, Marylanders, or New Yorkers do? Well, of course they would. But they are not willing to do the one thing that would make that pay possible—move to Los Angeles, Baltimore, or New York City—because they know they would not really be better off as a result. They know that national labor markets will not allow them to enjoy a small-city or rural lifestyle *and* earn big-city wages. They have to make a typical economic choice and trade off one in pursuit of the other. In fact, far from leaving Montana to seek greener pastures elsewhere, in the first half of the 1990s workers poured in. Apparently, despite last-place earnings, people found that the standard of living in the state was quite high.

Paradoxically, many Montanans think that the movement of workers into and out of the state is symptomatic not of economic vitality but of stagnation. This is because they believe that the in-migrants and the out-migrants are very different people. In this view, typical out-migrants are young couples with families who are forced to leave the state in order to earn incomes that will "make ends meet," and in-migrants are older, well-established, relatively affluent people who can afford the luxury of coming to Montana to "eat the scenery." If that is true, then for an important and vulnerable part of the population, low earnings in Montana are not made up for by a high quality of life, and survival requires leaving.

This view is largely a matter of misperception. Young people do leave, of course, to the consternation of their families. And some newcomers are affluent, as their homes, cars, and clothes make abundantly clear. But these highly visible examples disproportionately color perceptions of migration in general. Christiane von Reichert (1998) has shown that compared with the population at large, the people coming to Montana are much younger (migrants everywhere tend to be young), somewhat better educated, and roughly equally affluent. In other words, they seem to fit the typical anecdotal description of the out-migrant who, it is said, has no choice but to leave.

Are Montana's out-migrants and in-migrants really much different from each other? It is hard to tell because little systematic information is available on the people who leave. But a telling fact regarding the ages of migrants is this: if we follow a particular cohort of children over time, any change in number in the cohort we observe will be principally due to net migration. In the case of Montana, these changes indicate that during the 1990s, there was a net in-migration of school-age children.[17] Evidently, if there were young couples who were driven from Montana by inadequate earnings, there were even more who believed that the standard of living made the state an attractive place to move to with their children.

WHY *DID* RELATIVE AVERAGE PAY AND INCOME DECLINE IN THE MOUNTAIN WEST?

We return to the issue discussed at the end of the previous chapter: how average real pay and income in the Mountain West could decline more (or grow more slowly) than elsewhere in the country. Apparently something particular to the region was taking place that national trends could not explain.

First, recall that most of the decline relative to the rest of the country took place during the 1980s. After that, the pay and income gap largely stabilized. Recall also that during the period 1978–1982, average real pay both in the Mountain West and in the United States as a whole declined precipitously as the country stumbled through two back-to-back recessions. The gap between the region and the country was created when average pay fell more steeply in the Mountain West during those recessions and, more important, did not rebound during the rest of the 1980s as it did in the rest of the country.

During that period of decline and subsequent stagnation in average pay, there was significant ongoing net in-migration into the Mountain West. As depicted in figure 5.5, that influx of new residents was especially rapid during the first half of the 1990s, when the pay and income gap relative to the country reached its high point. Despite the growing gap, on net almost 3 million new residents moved into the region during the 1980s and 1990s. This ongoing influx of new workers into a region where pay was already low maintained downward pressure on earnings as the newcomers competed with existing res-

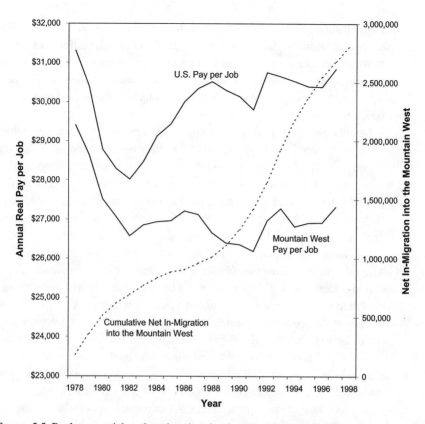

FIGURE 5.5. Real pay per job and net in-migration into the Mountain West, 1978–1997. Despite the growing gap in real pay per job between the region and the country as a whole, cumulative net in-migration exceeded 2.5 million people. *Source:* Bureau of Economic Analysis 1999 and U.S. Census Bureau 2000b.

idents for jobs. As the economy recovered from the recessions of the early 1980s and entered a period of extended growth, the upward pressure on real pay experienced elsewhere in the country was undermined in the Mountain West by the ongoing in-migration of new workers.

CONCLUSION

In this chapter, we have shown that there are large differences in individual earnings among states and that economic reasoning suggests that these differences serve to compensate individuals for geographic differences in cost of living and quality of life and compensate firms for geographic differences in the cost of doing business. The compensating character of earnings differences means that even though earnings differences are large, they do not imply that there are large differences in standards of living or real economic well-being. Migration is a process that tends to equalize standards of living across state lines and among urban areas.

Our analysis of pay and cost-of-living differences between metropolitan areas that are very large (populations of 2 million or more) and those that are relatively small (fewer than 500,000) shows that most of the large apparent difference in average pay disappears when adjusted for differences in cost of living; adjustment reduced a 44 percent gap in earnings per job to 10 percent. We also presented evidence indicating that the economic value of the social and natural amenities available in cities falls as city size rises, with a difference between large and small cities equal to about 20 percent of earnings per job. The combination of these two factors is more than sufficient to eliminate any additional economic well-being that might be conferred by the higher earnings available in larger urban areas. Calculated equilibrium earnings by state confirm that there do not appear to be real differences in well-being among the states.

We believe that the relatively low earnings in the Mountain West exist because of, and are compensated for by, substantial public, environmental, and social amenities. Mountain West residents earn less than the national average because they live in smaller cities, towns, and rural areas. In fact, when westerners are compared with other Americans living in communities of similar size, the difference in earnings disappears entirely. People living in small communities accept lower earnings because by doing so they can enjoy amenities not available in the country's larger metropolitan areas. The level of earnings sufficient to attract and retain residents in a state is lower when the proportion of the population living in rural areas is larger.

It is important to note that if residents choose lower incomes voluntarily, it is not reasonable to consider them economically deprived as a result of that choice. We might as well argue that all purchases consumers make must leave them worse off because such purchases require that they sacrifice part of their income. In general, voluntary trade-offs leave economic actors better, rather than worse, off.

A careful analysis of the relative earnings of individual Montanans shows that the penalty for living and working in Montana is highest for those most able to move to better opportunities if they were to choose to do so: the well educated and well paid. But rather than provoking an exodus, low earnings in Montana in the 1990s were accompanied by rapid in-migration of young workers and their families who were prepared to enjoy the state's unique quality of life.

Despite low earnings, the Mountain West is neither a uniquely nor generally disadvantaged region. But it is important to realize that in the Mountain West, as in the rest of the country, there are disadvantaged, distressed, and impoverished families, including many with children. In addition, there are local economies that are in serious difficulty, unable to continue to provide their residents with reasonable livelihoods. Our point is neither that everyone is prosperous nor that there is no role for public economic policy to play in helping individuals, families, and communities cope with economic disadvantage and disruption. Rather, our point is that whole regions such as the Mountain West or all of non-metropolitan America are not in the midst of an economic crisis that calls for drastic public intervention. Appropriate public economic policies must be far more selectively targeted on particular places and people and tied to an accurate understanding of how local economies operate, embedded as they are in a national economy with very mobile people, firms, and capital.

NOTES

1. These metropolitan areas were Fayetteville and Little Rock. Population figures for states and metropolitan areas are for 1996 (U.S. Census Bureau 1999b, tables 42, 43).
2. It is assumed that workers in Los Angeles and Boise have equivalent qualifications and that housing in the two cities is of equivalent quality.
3. Obviously, most of the adjustment would occur in Boise because relative to the size of the local labor force, the flow of migrants would be large there and small in Los Angeles.
4. In fact, empirical studies indicate that this is likely to be the case. More densely settled locations do have cost advantages for producers. Labor productivity rises (and per unit labor costs fall) as the density of settlement rises. In the Mountain West, population density in every state but Colorado is below the national average; average labor productivity is below the national average in every state except Nevada and Wyoming (Ciccone and Hall 1995). At the same time, as we discuss later in this chapter, quality of life deteriorates and cost of living rises as city size increases. Theory then suggests what in fact is the case: as city size increases, average pay and income rise.
5. Economists have elaborated the theory of local wage and rent differentials in numerous studies. See, for example, Beeson and Eberts 1987; Evans 1990; Harrigan and McGregor 1993; Roback 1982, 1988; Voith 1991.
6. Each point in figure 5.2 represents a metropolitan area. Population is plotted on a logarithmic scale, which means the horizontal distance between any two points measures the ratio of, rather than the absolute difference in, their populations.
7. For the period 1978–1997, the average annual *absolute* percentage difference in earn-

ings per job between non-metropolitan areas in the Mountain West and in the rest of the country was 3.8 percent. For the period 1985–1997, this figure was 1.6 percent.

8. This is true even in Montana, where earnings per job are the lowest in the region and among the lowest in the country. But in 1996, Montana was also the least metropolitan state in the country, and this large preponderance of rural areas and small urban communities accounts entirely for the gap between state and national earnings.

9. Because cost of living can vary within large urban areas, this procedure carries some risk of error.

10. The simple correlation coefficient for cost of living with pay per job is .572, that for population with pay per job is .694, and that for population with cost of living is .597.

11. For a discussion of these studies and the methods employed, see Freeman 1993, chap. 11.

12. The QOLI estimates are per household; the pay data are per job. In 1980, there were 1.4 jobs per household. If the $600 is expressed in terms of average household pay, it is about 14 percent.

13. Suppose, for example, that the actual difference in earnings per job between Montana and California is $10,000, but the difference in equilibrium earnings per job is $12,000. The latter figure represents the earnings difference that will stop Californians from moving to Montana; when the earnings gap reaches that point, it is just offset by differences in the amenities available in the two states. This amenity difference is then worth $12,000 and is understated by the observed, actual difference of $10,000.

14. Points representing four states that appear not to conform with this relationship are labeled in figure 5.4. Three (Florida, Arizona, and Nevada) are highly metropolitan states with low equilibrium earnings; these are states with high climatic amenities. One state, Alaska, has a large non-metropolitan population and high relative earnings; because of the state's high cost of living, these earnings are probably overstated. Excluding these four states, the correlation coefficient between the percentage of population in non-metropolitan areas and the equilibrium wage is –.61.

15. We used pooled data from the March Current Population Survey for the years 1991–1994, 1996, and 1997. This survey, conducted by the Census Bureau, provides information about earnings and selected personal characteristics of all adults in surveyed households. For a complete account of this analysis, see Barrett 1998b.

16. The notion of a "typical" gender, marital status, or occupation may seem odd. In the earnings function, gender is represented by a variable whose value is set at 1 for males and 0 for females (or vice versa; the choice is arbitrary). The "typical" gender of the individuals in a sample is then simply the average value of this variable for the sample.

17. For example, if there were 100 five- to ten-year-olds in the state in 1999 and 110 six- to eleven-year-olds in 2000, the increase would be due to net in-migration of 10 (or a slightly larger number because there is some—but very little—mortality in this age group). The fact that there was net in-migration does not necessarily imply that the total number of school-age children was rising. If successive cohorts entering the population are getting smaller, the total population can fall despite in-migration. For a complete description of this analysis, see Power 1998.

CHAPTER 6

Trapped in Images from the Past

Perception and understanding of the economic health of the Mountain West region and its residents matter when it comes to development of public policy. They matter a lot. Seeing an economic crisis where there is none can lead to all sorts of mischief.

Even an imagined crisis needs to be explained, and the story told to explain the crisis of the Mountain West goes forward by leaps of faith. Surely, every economy has a base. Clearly, the base of the Mountain West economy is its natural resource industries. Obviously, if natural resource industries are in trouble, so is everybody else. Even if this is not true, it seems to make sense.

It is with this story that the political and, ultimately, the economic mischief begins. Extraction and processing of raw materials unavoidably require access to publicly owned natural resources and inevitably have significant effects on the environment. This means that the profits of natural resource industries are directly affected by the public policies that determine what environmental protection and access to natural resources will cost. Inevitably, the private interests of natural resource firms come into conflict with the public interest in conservation and environmental quality.

In this situation, an international mining company, for example, will have a hard time making a compelling case for access to a particular publicly owned mineral deposit or for the right to pollute clean air and water simply because it could make a lot of money in the process. The mining company's claim on public resources is considerably strengthened, however, if it can wrap that claim in the public interest. Tying an imagined crisis in the regional economy to the collapse of its putative natural resource base helps the mining company do exactly that. What would otherwise be a group of private investors seeking access to public resources becomes instead an offer that a community "cannot refuse," an offer to rebuild its failing economic base and provide highly paid jobs to lift the area out of poverty.

It is not just the natural resource industries that wrap their private interests in the public interest in this way. Those who own commercial resources that are hard to duplicate—a particularly well located patch of real estate, a state-controlled liquor license, or a business in a downtown redevelopment district, for example—usually will profit by any quantitative expansion in the local economy. Growing population, employment, and total income increase the demand for the resources they own and hence their value.[1]

On the other hand, simple growth in the local population or in business sales does little to improve the well-being of the community at large. On the contrary, with increased congestion and a rising cost of living, most local residents may well be worse off. It therefore behooves the owners of local businesses that gain from growth to blur the line between public and private interests by arguing for the need for more jobs and income in order to battle economic collapse and growing impoverishment. Local chambers of commerce are usually quite successful at this ploy, often becoming the primary interpreters of local economic mysteries and providing definitive statements on local economic health.

In these situations, misunderstanding of the local economy tends to distort public decision making. Most people value both economic opportunity and such local amenities as schools and other public services, clean air and water, open space and scenic beauty, and opportunities for outdoor recreation. In choosing where to live, people regularly sacrifice the higher income they might earn elsewhere for the public amenities of the place where they finally choose to settle. These choices are classic economic decisions: given limited resources, people choose the mix of market and non-market characteristics they regard as best for their families and themselves.

Belief that the economy is in a crisis when in fact it is not means that these economic decisions will be grossly and irrationally misinformed. The implicit message is that good public services and high environmental quality would be nice, but they are simply too costly. Collective economic survival is at stake; the "luxuries" have to be abandoned. If that were really the case, such trade-offs *would* have to be considered. But when the premise is false, people are encouraged to sacrifice public goods that are vital to their well-being, such as clean air, better schools, or stable natural landscapes, for something that serves only the narrowest private interests. This is bad public economic decision making. When anxiety and misunderstanding displace deliberation and careful analysis, the quality of public discourse and decision making deteriorate even further. The net result is that almost everyone is left worse off.

Mischaracterization of the local economy poisons the political and social environment in ways that go well beyond bad public policy. Because it is environmental laws and regulations that are likely to constrain natural resource industries and, therefore, the purported recovery of the economic base, the discourse on local economic development tends to take on a strong anti-environmental tone. And because it is government that is charged with protecting the environment, efforts to relax environmental restrictions in the name of economic revitalization often take on an anti-government tone. The "wise use" movement, heavily financed by natural resource industries, is a good example.

Anti-government sentiment rests on the conviction that the U.S. government, in protecting the environment and conserving the country's resources, has gutted the local economies of the Mountain West. As ill conceived as this conviction may be, in many places in the region, particularly in natural resource–dependent rural areas, intense hostility toward government spills beyond the confines of politics, pervading the social and personal lives of communities and creating a niche from which socially toxic hate groups can operate.

Misunderstanding of the economy can lend plausibility to even the most paranoid of anti-government delusions. Consider, for example, the odd conviction espoused by the "militia" and "freeman" movements in rural areas of the Mountain West that the ultimate purpose of federal environmental and resource policies is not at all to protect the environment. It is, rather, to advance a larger plot to squash self-governing rural communities and drive people off the land and into large cities, where their guns can be confiscated and they can be thoroughly controlled. Obviously, the vast majority of the region's residents would reject the paranoia implicit in this sort of conspiracy theory. But very few would reject the theory's economic premise that rural areas depend for their existence on the exploitation of natural resources.

The premise, as we have shown, is false. All across the Mountain West, rural areas, towns, and small cities have ballooned with new residents, and local governments have had to wrestle with the problems of growth rather than the problems of decline. And throughout this process, the shares of local income and employment generated by natural resource industries have been steadily shrinking. The economic future of the rural Mountain West does not rest in the hands of federal environmental bureaucrats; that so many can believe it does is a testament to the power of economic misunderstanding.

UNDERMINING CHOICES AND VALUES

It is not just the political decisions members of a community embrace that are distorted when they misunderstand the workings of the economy that surrounds them. The quality of the decisions and commitments they make, and the individual and social values that inform those decisions and commitments, are all called into question as well.

One reason incomes are relatively low in the Mountain West is that residents have consciously sacrificed income in exchange for access to non-commercial public goods. This sacrifice reflects a conscious understanding that economic well-being is tied not only to the consumption of privately acquired goods and services but also to shared enjoyment of public amenities and services. The substantial sacrifice in income that residents of the region are prepared to make is a striking indicator of just how valuable, and how vital to community health, these collective amenities are. When combined with a higher quality of life, lower incomes are a sign not of failure but of strength: they are an indication that people understand their own needs, that they share those needs with their neighbors, and that together they have provided for them.

When low incomes are mistakenly taken as evidence of economic failure, both the rationality and the values of the region's residents begin to appear questionable: residents are either fools or failures for continuing to reside in a poor and failing economy. They have made a bad deal and should welcome any proposal that promises them, however hollowly, more jobs and higher pay, even if it means sacrificing the very things that brought them to the area and hold them there.

Treating the growth in part-time employment as a sign of economic failure also suggests that people do not really know where their own best interests lie. The vast majority of people who work part-time do so out of choice, because they have other important obligations or interests to pursue. Just as they sacrifice income in order to enjoy public amenities, people sacrifice full-time wages so they can do things that are important to them: take care of their children, volunteer in the community, or maybe just go fishing. It is their call: they recognize that both work and leisure contribute to their own and their families' well-being. Preferences for work or leisure vary from one person to another, and the economy that accommodates these diverse preferences should be judged a success rather than a failure.

None of this is meant to deny that many workers and families in the Mountain West are in genuine distress because they cannot find enough employment and are not paid well enough for whatever jobs do come their way. What is important is to keep legitimate concern for those who are in fact economically deprived from being diluted and confused by treating *any* reduction in income or *any* part-time work with undifferentiated alarm.

When people voluntarily sacrifice income and full-time employment because they deem other things more important, their judgments should not be second-guessed, and the people themselves should not be considered failures or objects of public concern. To do so distorts efforts to help those in genuine distress by diverting resources into general economic development campaigns that primarily benefit well-to-do special interest groups.

WHY DO RESIDENTS BELIEVE THE MOUNTAIN WEST IS POOR?

Throughout the preceding chapters, we have described the economy of the Mountain West in terms that might be considered unconventional but that we believe are strongly supported by the factual evidence. At the same time, we realize that many residents, especially the region's political leaders, perceive the economy much differently and with far greater alarm. This is obviously disturbing, and the question we seek to deal with in this section is why. After all, more than once we have emphasized the importance of respecting people's perceptions, values, and choices. Like most economists, we assume that people are not generally ignorant or confused but instead act rationally on the basis of reasonably good information. There is usually a logic that can, at least in part, account for their behavior. If that is true, how can so many people hold a view of the regional economy that is so much at odds with the facts?

Real Nationwide Economic Distress

It is not surprising that by the end of the 1980s, most workers in the Mountain West could conclude that the economic opportunities available to them had deteriorated badly. They had. But the problem was not only regional. It afflicted the country as a whole, and it went well beyond a simple, short-term, recession-induced decline in average wages.

In the mid-1970s, real wages for the majority of workers began to decline, and they did not begin growing again—slowly—until the 1990s. Productivity growth stagnated, and the benefits of whatever growth there was flowed almost exclusively to the more skilled and educated minority. For young, less educated, and poorly skilled male workers in particular, earning opportunities deteriorated catastrophically. Since World War II, unionized manufacturing jobs had provided these men with a blue-collar path to a middle-class lifestyle; even high school dropouts with appropriate work habits could earn relatively comfortable wages. All that began to unravel as earning opportunities for such workers fell toward a minimum wage that was increasingly eaten up by inflation. And partially as a result of this deterioration in the opportunities available to young men, the number of female-headed households rose. The demands of raising a family combined with the limited employment opportunities available to unskilled, less educated women triggered an increase in child poverty rates.

The Mountain West, linked as it was—and still is—to the national economy by the mobility of goods, labor, and capital, experienced all these distressing developments, and residents of the region accurately perceived that something was going quite wrong. Where they were mistaken, however, was in believing that the problems they perceived were local in origin and could be solved by changes in local policy. Ignoring the open character of the economy, they concluded that if pay was low and falling, it had to be a result of sluggish growth in local employment and the loss of good jobs. And if income was lower in the region than in the rest of the country, then surely residents were not living as well as other Americans.

As we have tried to show, this leap from the right perception to the wrong conclusion was possible because people had a deeply ingrained but seriously flawed understanding of the regional economy.

Change Hurts or, at Least, Disorients

For most people, dealing with rapid or profound change in the economy is a tough proposition. Often, people's lives are disrupted when they are forced to make costly moves from one job, or place, to another. Even if they are not personally affected in this way, they know there is always the risk that they might be.

The very idea of losing a job they have been committed to for years, and having the skills and experience built up over those years wasted, is depressing and threatening. Abandoning one career to establish another, reentering the labor market in hopes of convincing a prospective employer that they have valuable skills and abilities and are not simply "losers," joining people half their age in a classroom to learn new skills—all this strikes at their confidence and self-respect. On top of it all is the question of how they will provide for themselves and their families as they navigate an uncertain transition to an unknown outcome. Ultimately, they and their families may have to cut their roots to one place and relocate to an entirely different part of the country.

These wrenching transitions and the anxiety they provoke are likely to be particularly acute when, as happened in many communities of the Mountain West, industries that were once the mainstays of local employment decline and are replaced by new and very different activities. The economic base on which the community has depended is replaced by something unfamiliar and seemingly insubstantial. As a result, even if the community is growing, and to the outside observer shows every sign of economic vitality, longtime residents will see and feel economic decline. They will find the hustle and bustle associated with new economic activity largely irrelevant because it offers no opportunities of interest to them.

GHOSTS FROM THE PAST: THE CULTURAL PERSPECTIVE

This reluctance to find opportunity in change is understandable, given the natural human tendency to rely on personal experience in interpreting economic events. But other elements conditioning the public's perception of the economy are more cultural in character.

The View through the Rearview Mirror

One such element is the public's shared understanding of just what constitutes the local economic base. This understanding is almost always retrospective. Children learn from their parents and grandparents what it was that brought people to the community and supported them as they put down roots. Activities become acknowledged elements of the local economic base by virtue of having been around for a long time.

The visible presence of large factories, open-pit or underground mines, farmland and ranch land, or surrounding forests often shapes, but also distorts, the way a community understands its economic base. New economic activity, because it often takes place in small firms and anonymous commercial buildings, is hard to see, and its contribution to local economic vitality harder yet to appreciate.

Relying on informal economic histories and casual visual inspections of the commercial landscape, residents of the community arrive at an understanding of the economic base that is inflexible and misleading. Looking at the local economy through the rearview mirror, they are likely to see economic decline. The industries that once sustained them are now mature and must cope with stiff global competition; to survive, they must adopt technologies that steadily reduce employment. It is a frightening image.

Culture and Custom

The attachments people form to their work are not just narrowly financial. Rather, work helps define a worker's personal identity and role in the community. As individuals become good at what they do, learn to enjoy it, and become proud of their accomplishments, they come to regard their work as an integral part of a satisfying way of life they would like to be able to pass along to their children. The larger community as well often identifies with and deeply appreciates the work that sustained generations before them and helped define the community's character. In the Mountain West, ranching, farming, mining, and logging are not just ways to make a living. They are ways of life.

Even if it is economically inconsequential, the decline of a community's historical base can threaten its identity, character, and familiar customs, and the resulting sense of loss will not be dispelled by the prospect of even the most profitable engagement with the new economy—"Sorry, we've been to Silicon Valley, and we didn't like it there."

The issue is not just a way of life; the new jobs themselves are repellent. As the economy swings away from the production of goods and toward services and trade, workers must move out of jobs that produce a palpable physical product and require skill, strength, and risk taking and into demeaning service jobs that require only appropriate subservience and produce nothing a worker can point to and say, "I made that."

This representation of work in the new economy is, of course, grotesquely distorted. Service work runs the gamut from washing cars to decoding genes, and jobs in goods production include everything from designing industrial processes to picking rotten cherries off a packing house conveyor belt. But as we have repeatedly emphasized, in evaluating the labor market's performance, it is important to account for the diversity of workers' needs and preferences and not to second-guess them. There are workers who despise the jobs available in the new economy and will continue to do so regardless of how much they are paid to take them.

Of course, that does not make services any less valuable or central to economic development. Investments in education and technology development, both of which are provided by service industries, were the dominant source of growth in the national economy over most the twentieth century (Denison 1974, 1985). More recently, the overwhelming influence of computers on the personal, social, and economic lives of Americans derives almost entirely from the intellectual efforts of hardware and software designers and the services provided by a host of systems analysts, consultants, and technicians. In all this enormous welter of activity, the physical manufacture of computers plays a very small part.

If services are so important to the success of the modern economy, why are jobs in services bad-mouthed so frequently? Part of the answer is that services are often confused with the retail trade, in which pay is uniformly low and there are few career paths. It is also true that a lot of manufacturing used to be unionized and very well paid. Currently, however, much of manufacturing is not unionized and pays wages that are close to the minimum and indistinguishable from those in the worst of the non-goods industries.

Sexism

There is another aspect of the culture that helps explain the hostility toward employment in service industries. Goods production in the past was dominated by men. Men were the cowboys, went into the mines, felled the trees, manned the factories (except during World War II), and constructed the skyscrapers, highways, and family homes. What are now considered "good" jobs, jobs that can "support a family," until quite recently always went to men.

On the other hand, the jobs now commonly thought to be "lousy"—child care, retail sales, personal care, domestic service, unskilled office work, and the like—are those to which women historically were consigned. These jobs traditionally, and not coincidentally, also paid substantially less *because* women occupied them.

Some of the hostility toward the growth of services and the contraction of goods production arises from fear that these trends may represent an expansion of "women's work" and a contraction of "men's work." Ultimately, that would mean that men would have to take women's work, and for some men, at any rate, that is a dreadful prospect.

The origins of this particular strain of hostility toward service employment are obvious. Sexist denigration of the women who have historically occupied service jobs is allowed to undermine any rational economic assessment of the jobs themselves. Somehow, working with one's muscles, sweat, and testosterone to produce goods is considered economically superior to working with one's mind, hands, and heart to produce services.

MIXED EXPECTATIONS OF GOVERNMENT: THE EFFECT OF POLITICAL ATTITUDES

There is another reason why the people of the Mountain West share such a bleak assessment of the region's economy: more often than not, it is what they hear about. Earlier in this chapter, we argued that natural resource industries have a direct financial interest in painting as bleak a picture as possible of the region's economic health. Simply put, the worse people think things are, the more likely they are to accept the dubious propositions that natural resource development will save them and that government should do whatever is needed to bring that development about.

But it is more than simple self-interest that keeps visions of economic disaster dancing in people's heads. Political leaders, editorial writers, higher education officials, and even environmental organizations seem to share in the general alarm and the sense that government should do *something*. Just what, of course, is a matter of dispute; there is little unanimity on that score. But there is surprising agreement on the proposition that in almost everything it does, government should act first and foremost with its effects on the growth of the economy in mind.

It may seem obvious that this should be the case, and maybe it should. But the expectation that government should manage its affairs in the interest of commercial economic growth also reveals that Americans have developed rather asymmetric expectations of the private and public sectors. Economically speaking, business firms and governments all have the same job: they own and organize resources for various productive ends. But the ways in which they are expected to do their jobs are really very different.

When a national corporation—or any business—decides that it would be profitable to close down one of its facilities or lay off thousands of workers, people are shocked, saddened, and occasionally angry but typically resigned. The corporation's managers, after all, are simply responding, as all good managers must, to market forces. They have no choice; indeed, they are to be applauded for making the "tough calls," knowing where to "trim the fat," or making the business "lean and efficient." In the final analysis, businesses do not exist to create employment. Hiring workers costs money, and other things being equal, efficient management of the firm's *private* resources means hiring as few workers and incurring as little cost as possible.

Imagine, on the other hand, that a government agency makes a decision about the efficient management of *public* resources that leads to workers being laid off; say, for example, that the National Park Service decides to preserve the substantial public value of a unique natural landscape by prohibiting the use of snowmobiles, to the detriment of local snowmobile rental agencies, hotels, gas stations, and the like. In this situation, there will almost certainly be angry outbursts and calls for investigation and legislation to stop the government from "damaging the local economy."

What is going on here? Some may see this as simply a reflection of the difference between the dictates of an impersonal market, for which no one is really responsible, and a political decision that really did not have to be made and for which there is obviously someone to blame. But that is not true. The national and international corporations that dominate the American economy are bureaucratic organizations run by flesh-and-blood individuals who have the latitude to make judgment calls about what might be best for their careers, salaries, and stock options. On the other hand, most government agencies are constrained by laws and budgets; government managers cannot simply do what they want. Both are trying to provide valuable goods and services, and both, although they have some room to maneuver, face constraints that force them to make hard decisions. Yet we respond to those decisions quite differently, depending on whether they are public or private.

It is possible that this dichotomy is nothing more than a reflection of civic values. In a democracy, government is supposed to be responsive to citizens, who have a right to make their opinions known. In a private enterprise economy, citizens have no comparable right to tell managers or owners how to run their businesses. But it is hard to imagine that if they felt free to do so, Americans could plausibly criticize corporations for cutting employment. It is hard, on the one hand, to praise a business for figuring out how to do more with less and then, on the other, to condemn it for trimming its workforce.

Whatever the explanation, we hold public and corporate resource managers to different standards. Corporate managers are expected to use the resources at their disposal as efficiently and profitably as possible. Implicitly, at any rate, government managers are apparently expected to use the resources they control to maximize payrolls (in other words, labor costs) in the surrounding community, regardless of efficiency or the effects on the agency's primary policy objectives.

As the government seeks to protect or enhance air and water quality, wildlife habitat, open space, scenic beauty, and outdoor recreational opportunities, its efforts necessarily will have effects—some positive, some negative—on private economic activities. Government management of the natural resources found on public lands will have similar effects on the fortunes of private individuals who would like to use those resources commercially.

Those who believe they are harmed by these decisions, as the natural resource industries often do, can take advantage of the asymmetry in public expectations regarding public and private resource management by representing efficient government resource management decisions as nothing more than economic warfare waged on the local community. Such claims will resonate with residents, even though a comparable decision by a private firm to close a facility and lay off workers would trigger little protest and no heated talk concerning declarations of economic war.

This asymmetric attitude toward public and private decisions is not just a matter of political ideology. It is also important to local economic well-being. If publicly provided goods and services were of only minor economic importance, efforts to constrain the government in its efforts to provide them would not matter much to the local economy. But as we have demonstrated, residents of the Mountain West are willing to make substantial sacrifices of income in order to enjoy the amenities the region provides. Clean water and air, outdoor recreation, good schools, stunning landscapes, safe streets, and a host of other public goods are a source of immense satisfaction to people who choose to live in the region. If the government failed to protect and enhance the quality of these public goods, it would be compromising the well-being of citizens and could rightly be accused of mismanaging the public trust.

In conserving resources and protecting the environment, the government is doing more than simply providing public goods that are essential to the well-being of citizens. It is also providing for vitality and growth in the local economy. It is true that in particular instances, environmental regulations and resource management practices may make it costly or even impossible for private firms to function. But in the long run, it is the environmental quality such regulations seek to protect and enhance that attracts people to the Mountain West and keeps them there. All across the region, there are communities that are growing not because they are tearing up the ground or cutting down the trees but because they are *not* and as a result are very attractive places to live. The success of private interests in portraying such government policies as economically damaging and irrational is an important indicator of how confused public economic thinking has become.

NOTE

1. Businesses that can operate without access to unique resources are unlikely to experience the same gains from quantitative growth. As demand and profits rise, such firms face new competitors who will capture part of the expanding market and erode profits. The proliferation of videotape rental establishments in rapidly growing communities may be particularly illustrative of this process, but many established businesses have closed as a result of increased competition, even in very rapidly growing communities.

CHAPTER 7

What Should Be Done?

Appropriate Public Economic Policies for the Mountain West

During at least the last decade of the twentieth century, the economies of the Mountain West displayed remarkable vitality and growth, and despite their relatively low incomes, in relation to other Americans the region's residents are not economically deprived. These and other conclusions we have reached may seem optimistic to a fault. Do we mean to say that there is nothing wrong in the Mountain West? Are we implying that there is nothing government can do to help citizens enjoy a higher standard of living?

Decidedly not. The portrait we have painted of the regional economy is not intended either to hide or minimize the region's very real problems or to discourage creative public responses to them. Rather, we have simply sought to separate the wheat from the chaff. There is, after all, no point in expending time and effort in dealing with problems that are trivial or in crafting solutions that will not work or will even make things worse. It is important to establish some priorities, to deal first with the issues that are most pressing and that it is reasonable to think we can do something about.

THREE RULES FOR SOUND POLICY

What, then, are the problems that we think require the immediate attention of the people and governments of the Mountain West? We will get to that point shortly, but first we want to draw on the analysis in the previous chapters to outline what we consider to be three essential elements of appropriate and effective local economic policy.

In Policy Making, Modesty Is a Virtue

As labor, capital, and goods move across open economic boundaries, they forge a link between the local and national economies and form the pathways over which national economic forces overwhelmingly shape local economic developments. Openness and mobility mean that what goes on locally will largely be the result of events in the national economy. This vulnerability of the local economy to outside economic forces has an important implication for state and local governments: put bluntly, there is only so much they can do and a whole lot they cannot.

One of the most important things local government *cannot* do is raise wages or lower unemployment rates through employment creation programs. The idea is simple: if lots of new jobs are being created, the demand for labor will rise and the unemployment rate will fall or wages will rise or, it is hoped, both will happen. The problem is that the results will be temporary at best; as labor market conditions improve, workers will be drawn to the area and wages will fall, or unemployment rates will rise, or some combination of the two will occur. Strange as it may seem, high unemployment rates and rapid employment growth often go hand in hand (U.S. Department of Agriculture 1997; Marston 1985, p. 74).

Another limitation governments must recognize is the overwhelming influence of business cycles, price changes in international markets, and the life cycles of locally important industries. When the demand for local production collapses in a national recession, or the price of copper slides below the cost of extraction and refining, or the products and production processes of local industries become obsolete, there is not much hope that tax breaks or subsidies or wage concessions will undo the damage.

Finally, local governments should not beat their heads against the wall trying to prevent local business failures. Business failures are part and parcel of a market economy, and they are as common in thriving areas as they are in areas in decline (O'Sullivan 1993, pp. 161–162).

That there are such severe limitations on what government can reasonably hope to accomplish may seem discouraging. But the real lesson here is that local government should choose its targets carefully and should not take the blame for failing to correct problems that are beyond its control. In short, in the making of local economic policy, modest and realistic aspirations are a virtue.

The Public Interest Should Be Carefully Defined

The legitimacy of any public policy can be readily undermined unless the public interest that policy is supposed to promote is made clear from the outset. After all, if the use of public resources is at issue, public interests should be served.

This is of central importance because in general, Americans rely on private enterprise to organize their economic lives and pursue their private economic ends. Although citizens inevitably have some interest, large or small, immediate or distant, in the economic decisions that others make and in the market outcomes that result, the legitimate way to pursue most of those interests is through private market activities: investments, negotiations, contracts, and the like. If citizens used government to pursue their private interests in the outcomes of one another's economic decisions, private enterprise as the organizing force in the American economy would soon disappear. Simply because everyone is affected by market outcomes does not, in general, justify public market intervention.

Of course, individuals and businesses do nevertheless try to promote public policies that will serve their private interests. But because doing so is antithetical to the principles of a private enterprise economy, they must, as we have mentioned, represent their private interests as though they were those of the public at large. This leads to a great deal of obfuscation of what is actually at stake when any policy is contemplated. As a result, claims that particular policies will serve the public interest need to be evaluated carefully. Sometimes this is easier said than done.

Consider again the example of policies to promote more rapid employment growth. In most communities, it is an article of faith that creation of more jobs is in the public interest; so much so, in fact, that almost every policy initiative—even the construction of a playground or an art museum—comes accompanied by an obligatory toting up of the jobs the policy will create.[1]

And why not? Is there not a public interest in finding jobs for or raising the wages of people in the community? Of course there is, but as we have seen, in local economies, which are open to in- and out-migration, local job creation does not actually have those effects. If such policies do anything, it is probably simply to expand the size of the economy without boosting the pay of residents (with the exception, perhaps, of the new in-migrants) or the ease with which they can find appropriate employment. This means that rather than promoting the public interest, employment creation may actually damage it, when the costs of economic growth—congestion, escalating real estate prices, loss of open space, and the like—are taken into account.

It is possible to imagine a setting in which a plausible case could be made for public policies that support private job creation—for example, an isolated community from which underemployed workers find it difficult to depart and into which new residents are unlikely to move even if good jobs are available.[2] In such a community, job creation would tend to reduce unemployment and raise wages.

Besides workers and their families, there are other winners and losers in the employment creation game. As we have already mentioned, growth of the economy raises the demand for certain hard-to-duplicate resources, such as centrally located commercial real estate, and the owners of these resources benefit. Typically, as well, employment creation policies involve the offering of incentives to one group of firms at the expense of another group or the public at large. Thus, there is some income redistribution entailed in most public job creation policies. In some cases, redistribution may serve the public interest, as when, for example, it helps bring about what people consider to be a fairer or more equitable society. But before initiating a policy in the name of equity, it is important to know who the winners and losers are supposed to be and whether the policy will really affect the right people in the right way. In most cases, that is hard to do.

Economic Policy Should Focus on People Rather than Places

Our analysis of the pitfalls of employment creation programs suggests another important question about local policy making: in efforts to improve economic opportunities for local residents, should the target of public policy be the economic activity taking place within the local area, or should it instead be the individual economic actors currently living there? Put differently, should government focus on places or on people? The choice between the two comes down, again, to the question of mobility.

We take it as a given that to serve the public interest, local economic development policies must improve the lives of *current* local residents. They are, after all, the constituency of local government, and they provide the resources government must have to pursue its policy objectives. If the interests of this group are at stake, economic development policies that "work" not by raising current residents' incomes but in effect by replacing current residents with higher-income newcomers are obviously not accomplishing what they should.

If the local economy is open and mobility is high, the creation of new opportunities will attract an inflow of new residents whose competition will leave the wages, employment, and income of current residents largely unchanged. Even targeted efforts to bring in "good jobs" will have this effect: unless poorly paid local residents have the qualifications to take these jobs, it is not clear that any legitimate public objective will have been met. Place-oriented policies, then, will work only where mobility is low and local economic isolation has created a situation in which the abilities of workers and the jobs available to them are seriously mismatched. In practice, such situations are not common.

To enhance the economic opportunities open to current residents, then, the primary focus should be on *people,* specifically on improving people's ability to earn a good living through education, training, health, nutrition, and other human development programs. This has the advantage of ensuring that the benefits of local policies flow to local residents rather than to unknown in-migrants. Since relocating firms are particularly concerned about the quality of the available local workforce, developing a high-quality workforce makes the place a more attractive business location and increases the likelihood that when good new jobs are created, local residents will qualify for them. Most important, however, is the fact that when people move, which many inevitably do regardless of local economic conditions, the investment society has made in their development moves with them and continues to serve their needs wherever they find themselves. Public investments in local residents permanently enhance the economic opportunities open to them. Those investments are not lost or wasted, which is more than can be said about most public subsidies to private businesses.

Typically, economic development policies are judged to be successful if they result in higher local pay per job or higher per capita income. An interesting irony in this regard is that a place-oriented development policy that accomplishes nothing more than replacing impoverished current residents with well-heeled newcomers can appear to be quite a success. Even as perverse a policy as zoning poorer residents out of a community or driving them out with astronomical rents will make per capita income rise in a gratifying fashion.

On the other hand, a community that invests in the development of people may find that newly trained workers seek higher incomes elsewhere and that as they leave, they are replaced by new, low-income migrants. The result is that despite the improvement in the lives of what was the resident population, per capita income will not have changed and the policy will be judged a failure. Such a community could find itself confronted with a seemingly endless stream of in-migrants, all hoping to receive training, and an equally endless brain drain as those who have received training go off to seek their fortunes. If they really want to do so, people can help their poorer neighbors. But they have to realize that no matter how successful they are in that regard, they may never run out of poorer neighbors to help.

One place-oriented policy that *can* enhance the well-being of current local residents is the provision of public goods. As we have seen, people select a place to live not only for the income they can earn there but also because it offers a mix of amenities that they find particularly attractive. Providing more of those amenities will make them better off. Of course, it may also attract in-migrants and, as a result, reduce local wages. But because existing local residents can be expected to value those amenities more highly than later in-migrants would, the gains from improved amenities will outweigh the losses from reduced wages.[3]

WHEN GOVERNMENT SHOULD ACT

In the previous sections, we presented what we consider some important considerations to keep in mind when formulating local economic policies. These are that policies should be realistic and modest, should seek to promote clearly understood public interests, and should generally focus on people rather than places. We present these considerations to indicate not so much the limits of government as the possibilities. In particular, in this section we discuss three issues—poverty and inequality, management of the costs of growth, and public policy in regions in decline—that we think are of significant concern to the people of the Mountain West. They are issues that government can and should do something about.

Poverty and Inequality

One alarming feature of the economic transformation of the Mountain West is that it has taken place at the same time poverty and economic inequality have grown. Rapid expansion of the economy has been accompanied by the proliferation of many part-time and seasonal minimum-wage jobs that cannot possibly adequately support an individual, not to mention a family. Meanwhile, a new affluent class flaunts its wealth by building huge, prominently visible homes, driving outrageously expensive cars, shopping in exclusive boutiques, and frequenting restaurants that locals enter only through the back door, to wash dishes and bus tables.

Poverty, particularly poverty among children, is a focus of intense public concern, and government unquestionably can and should take a role in its reduction. But unfortunately, there is also a good deal of misunderstanding and confusion about the problem, and some policies that at first blush look attractive are bound to fail.

Using the Poor to Help the Non-Poor. In the Mountain West, concern for low-income households is used to justify the implementation of policies intended to create more high-paying jobs. The notion is that if such jobs were available, poorly paid individuals currently living in the region would take them and poverty would be reduced. However, it is clear that for this to work, the region's poorly paid workers would need to have the skills to perform those highly paid jobs. Moreover, the poorly paid jobs they abandon would have to stay empty; if they were filled again, a new group of poorly paid workers would replace those who had moved on.

None of this is likely to happen. As we pointed out in chapter 3, millions of relatively highly paid service and goods-producing jobs were created during the 1980s and 1990s in the Mountain West, but as discussed in chapter 4, they generally were not taken by poorly paid workers, and they did not reduce the number of poorly paid jobs. That is why, after a decade or more of leading the country in job creation, the Mountain West still has below-average pay. Typically, good new jobs were taken by highly qualified in-migrants rather than poorly paid local residents. Minimum-wage clerks, dishwashers, and room cleaners cannot take high-wage computer, business, and medical services jobs. Moreover, when local residents did move from low- to high-wage employment, the jobs they abandoned were filled by in-migrants, albeit those with fewer skills, who were willing to work for the same low wages. The outcome, in other words, was simply a larger low-wage economy and no fewer people in poverty.

The point is that policies aimed at job creation will do little to reduce poverty in a highly mobile, rapidly growing economy. Nevertheless, businesses and individuals with private interests in growth promotion and advocates for the poor who misunderstand how the labor market works continue to be proponents of growth as a solution to poverty.[4]

The Region Is Not the Problem. It would seem to go without saying that one reason *some* people are poor in the Mountain West is that apparently *everyone* in the region is short on income, at least in comparison with the rest of the country. After all, we have documented large gaps between the region and the rest of the country in per capita income and pay per job. If these gaps crop up all across the spectrum of pay levels, obviously some individuals and families in the Mountain West are driven into poverty by the fact that they live where they do. Our research, however, indicates that this is not the case.

In Montana, the state with the lowest pay in the Mountain West, the size of the hourly wage loss associated with living in the state grows with educational attainment and position in the wage structure. Well-educated and well-paid workers, in other words, sacrifice a significant share of their income to live in the state. At the other extreme, poorly paid and poorly educated workers sacrifice relatively little; they earn about as much in Montana as they would elsewhere. Why this is true is not completely clear. It may be that low-wage workers simply cannot afford to give up income to enjoy the benefits of living in Montana, whereas high-wage workers can. Also, because wages at the lower end of the distribution are supported by a nationally legislated minimum wage, there is a limit to how much sacrifice can be extracted from workers at the bottom of the wage structure. Whatever the reason, the critical implication is that when Montanans are poor, it usually is not because they live in Montana.

A corollary to this argument is that raising regional per capita income will not necessarily lift people out of poverty. If the income gap resides mostly at the upper end of the wage spectrum, closing the gap may have no appreciable effect at all on those at the lower end. As always, averages can be misleading.

Identifying the Low-Income Problems of Priority Public Concern.
One frustration of public and private organizations that seek to assist low-income households is that substantially fewer than half, often only one-quarter or one-third, of qualified households participate in their programs. Some of this is due to the admirable but possibly misplaced pride and independence of low-income householders. Some of it, however, is due to the fact that statistically defined poverty encompasses a complex, varied, and dynamic set of household circumstances.

Estimates of the poverty rate are derived from the Current Population Survey, which is administered nationwide every month by the U.S. Census Bureau. Because the number of individuals and families with poverty-level incomes varies substantially from month to month, the national poverty rate is calculated by averaging monthly data over a year; state and local poverty rates are calculated by averaging over several years.

In any given month, a household's income can be low for many reasons. A wage earner may be between jobs or taking time off to go to school or pursue other training. An owner of a new business may be struggling to get the business up, running, and turning a profit. Passing personal or family health problems may lead a worker to reduce his or her working hours. In contrast to these *temporary* causes, a household's income may be low in a given month for the same reason it has been low every month for an extended period of time: the householder's failure to find or hold a job with sufficient pay and hours. Regardless of the cause, all families experiencing low income are included when the poverty rate is calculated.

In the mid-1990s, about 20 percent of the U.S. population lived in families whose income fell below the poverty line for at least one month during the year, but only about 5 percent of the population fell below the poverty line continuously for twenty-four months or more. That is, the chronically poor represented only about one-quarter of all households that officially fell below the poverty line at some point.[5] The median duration of poverty was about four months (Naifeh 1998).

Chronic poverty is a much more serious problem than temporary poverty. Those who are temporarily poor often have savings to draw on or access to loans that allow them to maintain their level of expenditures at well above the poverty level (Lee 2000). Peter Gottschalk and Sheldon Danziger (1997) reported that 25 percent of families in the bottom income quintile in 1990 had moved to at least the second or higher quintile by 1991. Upward mobility is greater over a longer period of time; 46 percent of families whose average income was in the bottom quintile between 1968 and 1970 had escaped that position between 1989 and 1991.

Whether this is a lot of mobility or not and whether the income these families could potentially earn is adequate or not are matters of judgment. In any case, a significant share of the people who are poor today will not be poor tomorrow, and it is not clear that substantial public resources should be directed toward assisting them; there is good evidence that they would reject such support if it were offered.

The priority target of anti-poverty policies should be people who are chronically poor and those who have no resources to assist them, even during temporary periods of poverty. Whatever the size of this target group, trying to reach it through policies that speed up employment growth or "bring in good jobs" just will not work. Anti-poverty programs need to focus not on place but on people, and on the right people at that.

For instance, the chronic poverty rate among married couples in the mid-1990s was about 2 percent, whereas that among female-headed households was about 18 percent, almost nine times as great. Almost 40 percent of female-headed households had average annual incomes below the poverty line (Shea 1995; Naifeh 1998; Eller 1996). The high incidence of poverty in these households is the principal cause of the very high poverty rate among children. Reaching these households and the children in them is clearly a high priority.

One interesting aspect of the increase in family income inequality during the 1980s and 1990s is that a significant part of it resulted from differences in the total number of hours worked by the members of different families. Unlike the situation a century ago, when the poor worked longer hours than the affluent, by the 1990s families who enjoyed high incomes quite often did so only because they consisted of two very well paid professionals (and their children) who worked long hours. At the other end of the income distribution, there was a substantial decline in the number of hours worked by both young and elderly males. Some of this was the result of a larger percentage of young men continuing in school and an increasing incidence of early or partial retirement on the part of the elderly. But also important was a significant decline in the commitment of less educated young males to the labor market. Some had simply dropped out of the formal economy (Haveman 1996; Lee 2000). The limited employment opportunities and plummeting pay available to such workers no doubt explains much of this withdrawal.

Some part of the increase in inequality was, then, the result of voluntary decisions: on the part of the poor to forgo income in exchange for leisure and on the part of the affluent to forgo leisure in exchange for income.[6] To the extent that inequality increased for these reasons, it is of little social concern. On the other hand, if a significant number of potential workers are so discouraged by the range of economic opportunities that confront them that they abandon the formal labor market for the informal or illegal economy, there is reason for considerable concern.

The two low-income groups of priority concern, female-headed households and less educated young males, are, of course, not unrelated. The absence of family-wage employment opportunities for young males is one reason why they do not marry and take formal responsibility for their children. Nor are these problems easily solved.

For men, women, and children who have spent their lives under the conditions giving rise to hard-core poverty, the issue is no longer simply one of inadequate income and economic opportunity. The damage done by isolation from the formal economy and the experience of living in grinding poverty affect cultural values, physical and mental health, and social skills (Wilson 1987, 1997). If these effects are not dealt with directly, income supplements and expansion of economic opportunities will be of little help.

Our point, again, is that policies that simply seek to stimulate the overall economy, in hope that a rising tide will raise all boats, will not effectively solve the economic problems of priority concern. People are poor, and persistently poor, for complex personal reasons; the fact that in some cases they live in the Mountain West has virtually nothing to do with it. And if the Mountain West can somehow be made to grow faster or attract better jobs, poverty in the region will not go away.

Management of the Costs of Growth

The "resettlement" of the Mountain West has been under way since the 1970s. Because the region's original and erratic settlement proceeded in a series of "booms and busts" that left in their wake numerous forlorn mining, agricultural, and timber ghost towns, the blistering pace of economic growth today raises fears that the good times are once again just a prelude to the inevitable bust. With natural resource industries that were tied to the land disappearing and being replaced by ephemeral and footloose services and trade, the sense of economic vulnerability is even stronger. As a result, the Mountain West has been plagued by an ambivalence that has either paralyzed public economic policy or turned it in unproductive directions. The region that has been the fastest growing in the country for more than a quarter of a century spends much of its political and civic energy brooding over an impending decline instead of coping with the problems created by the ongoing growth.

In some circumstances, the problem is worse than this. When people think the economy is teetering on the brink of collapse, they may be unwilling to try to control the costs of ongoing growth. A community that is certain it is in imminent danger is likely to welcome uncritically any activity that promises to keep the economic ball rolling. It may not have the confidence to manage growth for the protection of local public values. Beggars, after all, cannot be choosers.

Although predicting the economic future is hazardous in the best of circumstances, the economic vitality of the contemporary Mountain West does not appear to be tied to the same kinds of passing economic enthusiasms that gave rise to the gold rushes, land bubbles, and energy booms of the past. Instead, it seems as firmly grounded in permanent settlement as was development during the last half of the twentieth century in southern California, Florida, Texas, and the rest of the Sun Belt (Cromartie and Wardwell 1999, p. 6).

In part, this is due to diversification of the region's economic structure. Dependence on natural resource extraction and development has declined and been replaced by a wide variety of non-goods-producing activities that can take place almost anywhere, particularly as the costs of communications and transportation fall. This diversity means that the region's economic eggs are not all in one basket; as a result, economic collapse is less likely.

The stability of the region is also supported by the high quality of life it makes possible. To a substantial degree, people have flocked to the Mountain West and economic activity has followed, rather than the other way around (Vias 1999). The region's growth is sustained by its attractiveness rather than by glittering opportunities to strike it rich (Rudzitis 1999; Nelson 1999).

In this regard, the attractiveness of the Mountain West as a place to live and engage in economic activity shows no signs of diminishing (Cromartie and Wardwell 1999, p. 6). Amenity-driven relocation of economic activity appears to be an enduring force shaping the region's future. This is not unique to the

Mountain West; the same force led to the suburbanization of metropolitan areas after World War II. Arguably, it was also part of what drove American settlement of the continent westward from the eastern colonies in earlier centuries.

Protecting Public Values. Although amenity-fueled growth in the Mountain West has proven remarkably robust, its sustainability is far from guaranteed. This is because, ironically, the economic vitality of the region tends to erode the quality of the natural and social environments on which it depends. The stress on social and natural systems caused by more people and more activity not only threatens to kill the goose that laid the golden egg. It also threatens the well-being of people who have made the region their home.

The obvious peril here is that if economic growth degrades natural and social amenities but fails to provide sufficient offsetting economic gains, residents will clearly be harmed. It is hard to know with certainty how people will assess these gains and losses. But because they have chosen to move to or stay in the Mountain West despite its relatively low incomes, it is safe to assume that most residents place a particularly high value on the amenities available in the region. That makes it likely that if they are forced to trade environmental quality for growth, they will come up short.

It is quite possible that there would be net losses to almost everyone. Natural and social amenities are public goods, which are likely to be overexploited and degraded by individual decision makers who have no private incentives to preserve them. The net result is something that none of the decision makers intends. If everyone wants to live amid open grazing lands with unobstructed views of the surrounding peaks, the open grazing land will soon disappear and the view will be blocked by new homes, which must be built ever taller to clear the roof lines of the homes that went before. And, of course, home building is just the start of the problem. So many people fish that nobody catches. So many people drive that nobody gets anywhere. So many people cozy up to their woodstoves that nobody can breathe.

Where public goods are concerned, it takes collective rather than individual action to pursue the preferred outcome. Without that collective action, everyone may be made worse off. In certain important and relatively common circumstances, the desired outcome cannot be achieved through private, self-interested decision making coordinated only by markets.

Mitigating the Costs of Growth. In order to protect the well-being of existing residents and the economic vitality of communities, it is essential that the most important public values be protected as much as possible as a community grows. This is far easier said than done, especially in the Mountain West, where a premium is placed on independence and a significant part of the population has resisted government authority since the early days of European settlement.

Providing guidelines for growth management is far beyond the scope of this book. But we do want to emphasize a few economic principles that are important in the development of a rational strategy to protect the public goods on which a community's character and well-being rely.

Our first principle is to end all subsidies to damaging practices and developments. A good deal of environmental damage is the unintended result of well-meaning government policies. Although Americans hold wide-ranging views on the appropriate role of government, both conservatives who wish to limit government and activists who want to protect public goods should be able to agree that the government should not subsidize private activities that damage other people's well-being. We have already discussed one type of government policy that falls into this category: publicly subsidized job creation. Given the lack of any public interest in growth for growth's sake, such programs gratuitously add to the pressure on the social and natural environments and leave communities worse off.

Somewhat more subtle is the way in which expansion of public infrastructure to accommodate new residents is financed. Often, the entire community is asked to share these costs, and there is an admirable community generosity in this arrangement; it is the way it has always been done. The community from its very beginnings has probably collectively provided roads, sewers, utility lines, schools, and police and fire protection to all citizens and shared the bill among both old and new residents, those with several cars and those with none, those with children and the childless, those with substantial property to protect and those who owned little. However, when this financing arrangement subsidizes rapid growth and sprawl that threaten community well-being, it makes no sense and should be abandoned. The simplest solution would be to insist that all residential subdivisions and commercial developments fund completely the infrastructure needed to serve them. A more sophisticated approach would seek to guide the provision of infrastructure subsidies to promote development that minimizes adverse effects on the social and natural environments.

Our second principle for protecting public goods is to make use of markets and contractual arrangements. Protecting public goods from overuse usually requires collective action, but that does not always have to take the form of restrictive regulations imposed by government. Governments can purchase residential and commercial development rights to protect open space or can purchase land outright to protect important natural area values. Private non-profit organizations can do the same thing, soliciting funds from those concerned about the natural environment, purchasing development rights, and then serving as trustee in the protection of those lands. Residential land developers can also seek to protect some of the environmental amenities home owners value by purchasing surrounding open space and clustering housing development to maintain natural area values. Alternatively, developments can impose restrictive covenants that prevent subdivision of individual lots; limit the size, height, and character of buildings; and limit the commercial uses to which the land can be put. Government land use planning regulations can support such private, environmentally oriented planning.

Our third principle is to develop a community vision and to plan ahead. Growth management can be effectively implemented only when the people of a community share a vision of what they want the community to be, understand the values at stake and what they stand to lose, and see the logic of the regulatory strategy that will get them where they want to go.

Without this shared vision and understanding, land use regulation is easily painted as a government power grab that strips people of their property rights, and unfortunately, in many small cities and rural areas, the population is often predisposed to view government regulation in this way. Such communities have never felt the need for active government regulation in the past and, not infrequently, have been attracted to their sparsely populated settlements by a shared suspicion of government and a general desire to be left alone.

The difficulty of the task is compounded by the fact that it is important to look forward well ahead of actual development proposals. Once specific proposals are on the table and the wheels are turning, the legal and political difficulty of getting matters under control is much greater and the economic cost of trying to protect open space and natural area values gets astronomically high.

On the other hand, it is difficult to develop a community consensus about protecting the qualities of the surrounding countryside when development is not imminent. It is only when both citizen groups and local governments have the equivalent of public entrepreneurs with vision, skill, and energy that growth management is likely to be proactive enough to succeed.

Our last principle is that everyone should get out of the bad habit of talking about jobs. We have already mentioned the pervasive tendency to assess the economic value of public projects of virtually any kind in terms of the number of jobs they will generate. Leaving aside the fact that this bean counting is almost always badly done, the important thing to remember is that more jobs are not necessarily, not even usually, a good thing. Choosing public goods on the basis of the jobs they will create leads to bad decisions and debases the public values that truly sustain the community.

Public Policy in Regions That Are in Decline

Throughout most of this book, we have argued that the Mountain West has been experiencing expansion that is faster in some places and slower in others but is generally proceeding at a pace that has brought the whole region considerable economic vitality. As it turns out, this is not entirely true; the problem, in part, stems from how the region is defined.

If we could ignore state boundaries and define the Mountain West in a manner that is geographically somewhat more narrow than that of the U.S. Census Bureau, the assumption of ubiquitous growth would be essentially correct. Stretching down the backbone of the Rocky Mountains, on both eastern and western flanks, there is almost a continuous set of contiguous counties that experienced average or above-average population growth during the 1990s (U.S. Department of Agriculture 1998b, p. 49).

When the Mountain West is defined as the entire area lying within the borders of eight states, however, there is one major exception to this pattern: the eastern counties of Colorado, Montana, New Mexico, and Wyoming that are on or adjacent to the Great Plains. Not surprisingly, these counties' growth patterns resemble those of the Great Plains states rather than those elsewhere in the Mountain West (Rowley 1998). Within the mountainous parts of the Mountain West there are also a few scattered counties that have seen little growth or actual decline.

Counties in the region that have been losing population can be distinguished from those that have been gaining by several features. Most of the former have very low population densities and are heavily dependent on agriculture (Rowley 1998, pp. 3–4). Typically, these counties do not have the mountainous landscapes or recreational features that have served as natural amenities elsewhere in the region. There are also, scattered throughout the Mountain West, counties that were highly dependent on mining operations that subsequently shut down. In most cases, these counties continued to retain and attract population, but in a few instances shutdowns led to a general contraction; the Butte area in Montana (Silver Bow and Deer Lodge Counties) and the Silver Valley in Idaho (Shoshone County) are examples. Finally, there are a few quite isolated counties in the desert country of the Southwest that have seen slow population growth or declines.

It is reasonable to ask what public economic policy is appropriate in areas that appear to be in a state of ongoing decline. After all, it is certainly possible that policies that are inappropriate in steadily expanding economies do make sense in areas that cannot generate enough economic activity even to hold on to their existing population.

The most conservative, and some would say coldhearted and fatalistic, response to this situation would be to breathe a sigh of relief and simply enjoy the continuity and familiarity that goes with an economy that changes only slowly over time. Although the rapidly growing economies of the foothill and mountainous areas of the Mountain West are in the midst of rapid change that leaves little that is economically or culturally familiar, these declining counties exhibit considerably more stability. The decline that is taking place on the Great Plains is not a catastrophically sudden one but rather has been under way since the beginning of the twentieth century; the population on the rural Great Plains peaked in the period before World War I (Rathge and Highman 1998). Because this region was never industrialized, it has not had to wrestle with the major changes in industrial structure that have disrupted communities across the Mountain West and the rest of the country.

For some, then, doing nothing has a good deal of appeal. There are, after all, true conservatives who want local economies and communities to be what they always have been, and they can take the economic stagnation of the Great Plains as a demonstration of the cost of that kind of benign neglect. Some, especially when they consider the frenzy of change elsewhere in the Mountain West, may decide it is a cost they are willing to accept.

For those who ask what can be done, however, the answers about appropriate local economic policy are not much different from those we have outlined for the region as a whole. It is still true that the best thing that can be done for young people and the workforce is to invest in the development of their skills and abilities.

Given almost a century of declining economic opportunity on the rural Great Plains, it does young people and workers no favor to make costly public commitments to marginal firms that are looking for handouts but cannot guarantee results. It is far better to make commitments instead to preparing young people and workers to take advantage of economic opportunities wherever they find them. That may happen locally, but more likely it will require that they move to other parts of the country.

As sad as it is for parents to see their children leave, it is not clear that it is sad or bad for the children, who often enough revel in the chance to explore the world and make their own choices. Not surprisingly, many of those children who leave home in their youth to pursue a broader range of economic and cultural opportunities return to their home region when they can to raise their families. The majority of the in-migration into Montana during the 1990s, for instance, was return migration by people who had some prior connection with the state (von Reichert 1998). Similarly, a good deal of the growth in the population of the southeastern states after World War II was tied to the return of those who had left during the Great Depression and the war and wanted to go home again (Mills and Hamilton 1989, p. 45; Long 1975).

Public efforts to enhance and protect the quality of social and natural environments are also essential in declining communities, even though they may be perceived as putting intolerable burdens on fragile public budgets. Great Plains counties often are in decline because they do not have local qualities and characteristics that allow them to attract and hold residents. To allow the local social and natural environments to deteriorate can only make things worse and delay any recovery. Poor schools, run-down public and private infrastructure, polluted water or air, toxic waste deposits, or other threats to public health and safety simply dig the community into a deeper hole. The importance of local amenities can be seen clearly even on the Great Plains. The areas in that region that have been able to resist general decline are those with natural amenities that have allowed them to recruit population and economic activity despite declining opportunities in agriculture (Cromartie 1998). The Black Hills area of South Dakota is one clear example. Others include the counties along the major river valleys of the Great Plains.

When communities and economies are in decline, neither conservatives nor liberals seem able to resist the impulse to insist that the government "do something." Despite the assumption implicit in such calls to action that state and local governments can somehow control the course of economic events, in general that simply is not the case. As we have already noted, in these matters mobility and openness of the local economy severely limit the range of government action, and there is no use in pretending that the county commission or city council or the governor or state legislature can undo the damage done by national recessions, gyrating international markets, or sweeping transformations of technology.

There *are* things of great significance to our well-being and to the health of the economy that state and local governments have demonstrated they can do when they put their minds and resources to it. Education from day care through graduate school; solid, productive infrastructure; protection of public health and safety; preservation of irreplaceable natural and cultural treasures; and assistance for disadvantaged citizens while they make difficult transitions in their lives are all examples. Public economic policies that focus and expand on these familiar areas of local government responsibility present more than enough challenges to our communities and plenty of opportunities to make a productive difference.

NOTES

1. Whether or not these estimates of the jobs "created" by particular initiatives are reliable is another matter.
2. Indian reservations conform to this description in many respects. Mobility into and out of reservations is low, and economic conditions on reservations are typically significantly inferior to those in the surrounding area. To some degree, immobility is encouraged as a way of protecting traditional Native American cultures and ways of life.
3. The conclusion is based on the assumption that current residents place more value on unique local amenities that potential in-migrants would; if it were otherwise, the two groups would have switched places. Consider, then, an amenity that current residents value at, say, $100 per year and potential in-migrants value at $50 per year. If such an amenity is made available, in-migration will occur and begin to drive down wages. Migration will stop when average income has fallen by $50 because at that point, the amenity and the income loss will offset each other. Existing residents, however, will experience a net welfare gain of $50. For more on this point, see Power 1980, pp. 29–33.
4. There is evidence that rapid growth and low unemployment in the *national* economy can reduce poverty. But if poverty is endemic in the national economy, local efforts to reduce it with faster growth will fail in the manner we describe.
5. This definition of chronic poverty (twenty-four consecutive months below the poverty line) is arbitrary and presumably understates the dimensions of the problem. A family that is regularly in poverty, say, sixteen out of every twenty-four months and in the remaining eight months barely clears the poverty line might well be considered chronically poor. However labeled, the family's situation is obviously not good.
6. We need to reiterate one last time that by leisure we do not mean lying in a hammock and sipping piña coladas. We mean, rather, using time for something other than paid work. This can include child care, community service, or a host of other activities that are certainly not lazy and far from restful.

CHAPTER 8

⟨graphic⟩ Conclusion

        Throughout this book, we have sought to develop an alternative and, we believe, more accurate view of the changes in the Mountain West economy and their consequences for the region's residents during the last two decades of the twentieth century. The way people think about their local economies directs and colors the types of public economic policies they adopt and determines how effective they are in protecting the well-being of their communities and fellow citizens. For that reason, we end by summarizing the most important of our factual and conceptual conclusions.

AVERAGE PAY AND INCOME

During the 1980s, pay per job fell all across the Mountain West, and although there was some recovery during the 1990s, by 1998 real pay per job was less than it had been in 1978. In some cases, notably in Montana, the decline over the period was large.

    Although falling pay per job obviously signaled an erosion of earning opportunities, it nevertheless overstated to some degree how badly workers and their families were doing. This was true for a variety of reasons. One is that part of the decline in pay per job was the result of a growing preference among workers for part-time employment. Another is that by holding more than one job, workers can increase their earnings as individuals, even if each job pays less. In fact, pay per worker outperformed pay per job during those two decades.

And finally, income per capita rose steadily despite the decline in pay per job, both because non-employment income rose and because a larger part of the population was working. A large part of the population experienced much slower income growth as a result of inequality in distribution; during the period we studied, the distribution of income became more unequal both within the region and across the country.

The increase in the number of part-time workers during the 1980s and 1990s should not be seen as a sign of a deteriorating job market. About nine of every ten workers working part-time say they do so by choice. Part-time jobs allow people with family responsibilities to work outside the home, students to partially or fully support themselves while they attend school, and farm families to stay in agriculture by diversifying the family economy with off-farm work. On the other hand, an unknown number of workers, mostly young, poorly educated males, may choose to work few hours because they are discouraged by the quality and pay of the jobs that are open to them.

Multiple job holding is not always a sign of a poorly functioning economy. Although moonlighting is often seen as the default strategy of workers struggling to make ends meet, it is practiced with about the same frequency by workers at all income levels and for a variety of reasons.

Some people work full-time by holding multiple part-time jobs. Some workers no doubt prefer this strategy, whereas others have no alternative but to accept it; unfortunately, we have no information about how multiple part-time job holders fall out on this question. It is likely, in any case, that the fringe benefits available to these workers are inferior to those of workers holding single full-time jobs.

INDUSTRIAL STRUCTURE

The industries in which residents worked changed over the two decades we studied, but not as profoundly as in the country as a whole. Because the Mountain West was never as industrialized as the rest of the United States, the national shift away from manufacturing and other goods production did not affect the region as much as it did the country as a whole.

The distinguishing feature of the structural transformation of the Mountain West was a decline in natural resource extraction and processing. But in the mid-1970s, the time at which we began our analysis, natural resource industries already played only a small part in the regional economy (see figure 3.2). Because of that, the effect of their decline was minor.

The change in the industrial structure of the Mountain West appears to have mirrored and been driven by a pervasive national pattern in which jobs shifted from goods production to services and other non–goods production. Given this national pattern and its influence on the Mountain West, is unlikely that what happened in the region was the result of unusual state and local economic policies or federal management practices on extensive public lands.

Contrary to dire predictions, changes in the industrial structure of the Mountain West did not lead to economic collapse. Rather, during the period in which natural resource industries were contracting sharply, the region showed impressive economic vitality, leading the rest of the country in population and job growth.

CHANGE IN INDUSTRIAL STRUCTURE AND DECLINING PAY

Changes in the industrial structure of employment did not cause the fall in pay that occurred across the Mountain West during the 1980s and continued in some of the states, notably Montana, during the 1990s. If, after 1978, the share of jobs in natural resource industries or goods production had never declined (which would have required these industries to grow at the same brisk pace as the economy as a whole), 90 percent or more of the decline in average pay would have taken place anyway.

The decline in economy-wide average pay was due to downward pressure on pay in almost every industry. These pay declines were greatest in goods production, particularly in natural resource extracting and processing industries, and smallest in services and other non–goods production.

Changes in industrial structure, in general, did not lead to painful economic disruptions in workers' lives. Wage histories of workers in Montana reveal that they regularly changed jobs in the pursuit of better pay, especially after working in relatively low paid entry-level jobs. These dynamic characteristics of the workforce and labor market allowed changes in the distribution of employment among industries to be made relatively smoothly and painlessly over time.

Our study of hundreds of thousands of these histories indicates that during a period of ongoing change in industrial structure, workers found stable employment relatively quickly. The minority who interrupted a long history of employment in one industry to move to another tended to see their pay rise, not fall. Highly paid natural resource workers who changed industry were not forced into relatively low paid tourism and trade jobs; rather, they typically were able to find new, relatively well paid work in construction and other manufacturing. Finally, we found that shifts in the distribution of employment among industries did not accurately portray the types of job transitions workers were actually experiencing. That is because some of the rapidly expanding but low-paid sectors such as tourism and trade primarily drew on new entrants into the workforce to fill these jobs rather than existing, experienced workers.

Although workers appear to have moved about in the economy mostly voluntarily and *on average* to good effect, this was not universally true. A significant minority of workers who changed jobs found themselves worse off as a result.

WHY DID AVERAGE PAY DECLINE?

The declines in pay experienced across the region during the 1980s were tied primarily to two back-to-back national recessions, which together constituted the most serious economic downturn since the Great Depression. Although national in extent, these recessions hit rural areas and the Mountain West particularly hard. Rural America seemed to be the victim of a conspiracy of events: high interest rates stalled construction, and the timber industry shut down; tumbling energy and metal prices choked off energy exploration and development and shuttered mines and smelters; agricultural prices slid downward, and some areas were hit with droughts.

Falling pay was not, however, just the fleeting by-product of the business cycle. In the late 1970s, forces emerged in the national economy that drove a sustained decline in pay for most American workers, doubling back on the gains of the previous thirty years. A variety of explanations have been offered for this reversal of the American dream. One is that technological change and globalization of the American economy caused the demand for labor to twist away from workers with relatively little education and fewer skills and toward workers with more of these increasingly valuable assets. The resulting excess supply of less skilled and educated workers broadly depressed wages, with almost all increases in pay flowing to the more skilled minority.

The other explanation centers on the decline during the same period of what in the past were important wage-setting institutions: the percentage of the workforce covered by union collective bargaining agreements and the real value of the minimum wage. These trends were also national in scope, although many states in the Mountain West supported efforts to weaken labor unions and limit the effectiveness of minimum-wage laws.

IS THERE A MOUNTAIN WEST PAY AND INCOME GAP?

Although in real terms per capita income in the Mountain West grew steadily following the 1982 recession and pay per job, after falling for a decade, was largely restored during the 1990s, relative to the rest of the country both pay and income fell between 1978 and 1998. By 1998, there appeared to be a looming gap in both pay and income between the region and the rest of the country. But this gap largely disappears under closer examination.

Pay levels are positively correlated with community size: high in the country's biggest cities and low in smaller cities, towns, and rural areas. This means that in calculating and comparing average pay for the Mountain West and the country as a whole, it is important to take account of where people live. Residents of the Mountain West on average live in much smaller communities than do other Americans, and it is this difference that accounts for all the gap in pay between the region and the country. When the pay received by residents of the Mountain West's cities and rural areas is compared with that of residents in cities of similar size and other rural areas across the country, there is no gap. This is true even of Montana, which has the lowest pay in the country but also some of the smallest cities and one of the most rural populations.

Residents of the Mountain West earn relatively low incomes, then, because disproportionately they live in small communities. But this does not mean that they, or the millions of other Americans living in communities much like theirs, are economically deprived. On the contrary: like other Americans, they find that life outside the country's large metropolitan areas offers important compensations for low earnings and income.

RELATIVE WELL-BEING

A telling fact about events in the Mountain West during the 1980s and 1990s is that fueled by in-migration, population growth accelerated just as relative pay and income reached their low point. This tells us something about people's judgments regarding the well-being they derive from living in the region and also explains why rapid job growth in the 1990s did not allow pay to recover completely from its decline in the previous decade.

In a local economy, where there can be no controls on in-migration, new job creation leads to a larger population and workforce, not to higher pay. And if workers move to an area for reasons other than the level of pay, wages will be lower inside the area than they are outside. That is what happened in the Mountain West: workers migrated into the region to take advantage of new employment opportunities, and because of the region's attractions, they were willing to do so despite the low pay. As a result, the pay gap persisted.

This situation was not unique to the Mountain West. Across the country, small cities and rural areas had pay and income levels below the national average largely for the same reasons: the low cost of living and highly valued amenities of these places attracted and retained workers despite low earnings. The ongoing movement of people from high- to low-income states—including those of the Mountain West—reveals that people, "voting with their feet," judge that the regions to which they are moving, overall, are not economically deprived.

APPROPRIATE PUBLIC POLICY

These factual results have important implications for local economic policy, as discussed throughout the previous chapters:

- Public economic policy makers in the Mountain West should recognize that it is economic vitality that characterizes most of the local economies, not impending economic collapse. Residents of the Mountain West are not desperate beggars. In fact, they enjoy the luxury of expanding economic opportunities; vital, attractive communities; and spectacular natural landscapes. They have an obligation to be choosers, and to choose well.
- Policy makers must recognize the open character of local economies and the limits a mobile workforce impose on what local economic policy can and cannot control. In particular, public policy makers must recognize that local governments cannot manipulate local pay and income by subsidizing job creation.
- Policy makers must clearly define the *public* interest before acting. "More jobs and income" is not an adequate definition of the public interest. Action taken simply because public policy "ought to be doing something" will be ineffective or counterproductive.
- Local economic policy should focus on enhancing the ability of existing residents to earn a decent living rather than on trolling for additional employers with tax breaks or other subsidies.
- Local economic policy should treat the community's site-specific characteristics, both public services and the quality of the natural and social environments, as important determinants of both citizen well-being and local

economic vitality. This makes those public goods an important part of the local economic base.

■ Efforts to alleviate poverty should focus on the particular circumstances that limit chronically disadvantaged people rather than try to "boost" the overall economy in hopes that this will help the poor; it will not.

■ Public policy should stay focused on the present and the future rather than on some folktale version of the past. The Mountain West *is* in a *post-cowboy economy* and has been for many decades.

■ Local public policy should respect the choices citizens make to pursue objectives beyond simply earning a higher income or working more hours. The decision to enjoy a better living environment or spend more time outside the paid economy, even if it means earning less, should not be interpreted as impoverishing the community; it may well do the opposite as it strengthens families, improves individual and public health, and increases citizen involvement in community affairs.

Wallace Stegner, one of the region's most insightful writers, speculated in 1969 on whether, as the Mountain West moves further in time from its frontier past of violence and exploitation, there might emerge in the region a society with a set of values and policies that are a fitting match for its awe-inspiring natural landscapes:

> Angry as one may be at what heedless men have done and still do to a noble habitat, one cannot be pessimistic about the West. This is the native home of hope. When it fully learns that cooperation, not rugged individualism, is the pattern that most characterizes and preserves it, then it will have achieved itself and outlived its origins. Then it has the chance to create a society to match its scenery. (Stegner 1980, p. 38)

The rampant growth, environmental conflict, and bizarre and violent hate group activity that have marked the region in the decades since Stegner wrote tell residents of the Mountain West that they have yet to create the society he envisioned. The region's notorious individualism still fuels a suspicion of government and of social cooperation that often blocks effective action to protect the very things that are the reasons for inhabiting this place. In this book, we have tried to show that the people of the Mountain West can certainly afford to move in the direction Stegner hoped for. Whether they will do so remains far from clear. But as Stegner said, this region is, after all, "the native home of hope."

Appendix

Technical Notes

THE REGIONAL ECONOMIC INFORMATION SYSTEM AND THE CURRENT POPULATION SURVEY

Throughout this book, we make repeated use of data from the Regional Economic Information System (REIS) and the Current Population Survey (CPS). We also refer to the results of many other studies that relied on one or the other of these data sources.

The REIS reports data that are *establishment* based, that is, developed mainly from information extracted from regular reports by business firms and government agencies. One of the great advantages of the REIS is that it contains data for quite small geographic areas (counties and metropolitan statistical areas, or MSAs) as well as states and the United States as a whole. There are many data series for these areas, including population, jobs, labor earnings, personal income by major source, farm income and expenses, and transfer payments by major program. What is lacking in the REIS data is any information about the characteristics of the people holding these jobs, earning the income, receiving the transfer, and so forth. This makes it difficult to trace the association, if any, between the economic events occurring in a particular place and changes in the characteristics of the people living there.

The CPS, on the other hand, comes from monthly surveys of personal and household characteristics and economic situations of individuals and households across the country. These surveys allow researchers to trace the relationship between characteristics of a group of individuals and their economic condition. Because the CPS is national in scope, however, there are never enough individuals sampled in particular local areas to draw conclusions about those areas.

Neither the REIS nor the CPS, then, gives us everything we would like, but each is useful for some kind of analysis that helps shed some light on what is happening in the economy of the Mountain West.

COUNTING JOBS AND WORKERS

To understand the meaning of measures such as earnings per job, jobs per worker, and earnings per worker, it is essential to know how jobs and workers are counted.

During any year, periods of employment with a particular employer vary greatly in length, from a few days as a seasonal or temporary worker to the entire year for any regular full-time position. Although each of these periods can be called a job, they do not all count equally in calculating the total number of jobs available during the year. To see why, consider how job figures are calculated by the U.S. Department of Commerce's Bureau of Economic Analysis (BEA), on the basis of reports from private and government employers and from individual income tax returns. The BEA's reported wage and salary jobs for a single year are the average, over the year, of total monthly employment reported by all employers. If a single worker has more than one job, he or she appears on more than one employer's payroll during a particular month, and each appearance is counted as a job during that month.

Given the averaging procedure, a period of employment spanning all twelve months of the year counts for one job, but a period spanning only six months counts for half a job (a period lasting n months counts for n-twelfths of a job). In other words, total jobs reported in the data are *full-year equivalent jobs.* The BEA uses reports of self-employment income on individual income tax returns to compute the number of self-employment jobs; this information is reported on an annual basis, and again, each job is assumed to be a *full-year equivalent one.*

The number of workers in the labor force reported for a single year is also calculated as the average over the year of total monthly employment, but in this case each worker, even if he or she has multiple jobs, is counted only once. This averaging again means that the annual figure for the number of workers gives the number of *full-year equivalent* workers.

There are some important conclusions to be drawn from these measurement conventions. First, when we consider pay per job and pay per worker, we are, *to a degree,* standardizing for the amount of work the job involves or the amount of work the worker performs because each is measured on a full-year equivalent basis. For example, two jobs, one that lasts a month and pays $2,000 and another that lasts a year and pays $24,000, will both be recorded as $24,000 jobs (on an annual basis). This is obviously desirable: we would not want to say that the full-year job was twelve times better paid than the monthlong one.

The work required by a full-year equivalent job, however, is *not* standardized; rather, it varies with the number of hours worked per week. (Some variation could also come in the number of weeks worked per month; a job that involved one week of work per month would appear in the data as one full-year equivalent job. But because variation in weeks per month is not reported and we suspect it is relatively minor, we assume that such variation is negligible in our discussions of pay per job.) Similarly, the work performed by a full-year equivalent worker is not standardized because an individual working all year can vary his or her work effort quite a bit by varying weekly hours or the number of jobs held simultaneously. The upshot of all this is that pay per job and pay per worker do not measure the reward for a *fully* standardized amount of effort, although an important source of variation in effort—part-year or seasonal work—*is* accounted for.

The statistic for jobs per worker reflects the amount of *simultaneous* multiple job holding that workers are undertaking, but not *serial* multiple job holding. Workers moving from one job to another over the course of the year may say they held several jobs, but the number of jobs per worker reported in the data will be one. Again, this is obviously desirable; we would not want increased employment turnover to be reflected in the data as an increase in the number of jobs per worker.

INDUSTRIAL STRUCTURE AND WAGES
FOR DIFFERENT TYPES OF LABOR

There are two ways in which changes in the industrial composition of output can change the level and structure of wages. One is that industries paying high wage premiums can be replaced with industries paying low wage premiums (the opposite is also possible, of course, but that is not what is generally thought to be happening).

Another is that as some industries grow and others contract, the pattern of demand for labor of various kinds will change. For example, many U.S. industries that have lost ground to imports use unskilled labor intensively. As domestic production contracted in these industries, so did the demand for unskilled labor, and as a result, wages of unskilled workers fell. Competition spread this wage decline to all unskilled workers, whether they happened to be employed in the contracting industries or not. The result was a growing wage gap between skilled and unskilled workers but no gap between unskilled workers based on industry of employment.

Competition also spread the unskilled wage decline across regions and throughout the economy, making the change in the wage structure a *national* labor market phenomenon. For that reason, it is unlikely that changes in industrial structure at the local level by themselves will have a significant effect on wages; the effect of such local changes on the national demand for labor of various types is simply too small to make a difference.

It should be noted that although the gap between unskilled and skilled worker wages opened up substantially in the 1980s and 1990s, just how important expanded trade and exports of jobs were in opening the gap is disputed (Krugman and Obstfeld 1997, pp. 67–92).

DIVERGENT TIME PATHS OF INDIVIDUAL AND AVERAGE EARNINGS

For a variety of reasons, workers typically experience rising earnings in the course of their work lives; we can say that their earnings follow a rising *path* through time. How high the path is and how steeply it ascends depend, in part, on a worker's characteristics—education, occupation, and the like. Even if all workers are on rising paths, the average earnings for a group of workers can fall if (1) the relative number of workers who are at the starting (low) end of their paths increases, (2) the relative number of workers whose characteristics consign them to low paths increases, or (3) labor market conditions are such that new entrants into the labor force are starting out on lower paths than equally qualified workers started out on in the past. It is obviously only if average earnings are falling for the last of these reasons that we should be concerned; it would mean that workers entering the labor force today were facing lifetime earning opportunities inferior to those faced by their parents or other older workers.

EARNINGS FUNCTIONS

A typical earnings function may look something like the following:

$$W = a + b_1E + b_2A + \cdots + b_nX$$

where W is hourly wages, E is education level, and A is age, and these are followed by a list other relevant characteristics ending with X, which could represent, say, occupation. The term a is a constant, and b_1 and b_2 measure the change in W associated with a one-unit change in E and A, respectively. An important feature of $b_1, b_2, \ldots, b_n$ is that they measure the effect on W of a unit change in the variable with which they are associated, *other things held constant.* The values of $a, b_1, b_2,$ $\ldots b_n$ are derived statistically from data for a large number of workers and are not always applicable to specific individuals. Thus, for example, the data might indicate that other things equal, graduating from college raises the wages of a typical American worker by \$2, although this will not be true of all college graduates, among whom some will do better and others worse.

References

ACCRA. 1998. *ACCRA Cost of Living Index.* Vol. 31, pp. 1–4. Arlington, Va.: ACCRA.

Amirault, Thomas. 1997. "Characteristics of Multiple Job Holders, 1995." *Monthly Labor Review* 120 (3): 9–15.

Barrett, Richard. 1998a. "Industry Attachment and Change among Montana Workers, 1988–1996." Unpublished research report. Missoula: University of Montana, Department of Economics.

Barrett, Richard. 1998b. "The Montana Discount: Who Earns Less in Montana, How Much, Why, and What Can Be Done about It." Unpublished research report. Missoula: University of Montana, Department of Economics.

Barrett, Richard. 1999. "The Montana Discount: Analyzing the Sources of the State's Hourly Wage Gap." Paper presented at the Thirty-Third Annual Pacific Northwest Regional Economic Conference, Boise, Idaho, May 6–8.

Barrett, Richard, and Thomas Power. 1997. "Montana Workers' Labor Market Experiences during Industrial Transition: 1988–1996." Unpublished research report. Missoula: University of Montana, Department of Economics.

Beeson, Patricia E., and Randall W. Eberts. 1987. "Identifying Amenity and Productivity Cities Using Wage and Rent Differentials." Federal Reserve Bank of Cleveland *Economic Review* 3:16–25.

Bernstein, Jared, Elizabeth C. McNichol, Lawrence Mishel, and Robert Zahradnik. 2000. *Pulling Apart: A State-by-State Analysis of Income Trends.* Washington, D.C.: Center on Budget and Policy Priorities and Economic Policy Institute.

Blomquist, Glenn C., Mark C. Berger, and John P. Hoehn. 1988. "New Estimates of Quality of Life in Urban Areas." *American Economic Review* 78 (1): 89–106.

Bluestone, Barry, and Bennett Harrison. 1982. *The Deindustrialization of America: Plant Closings, Community Abandonment, and the Dismantling of Basic Industry.* New York: Basic Books.

Bound, John, and George Johnson. 1992. "Changes in the Structure of Wages in the 1980s: An Evaluation of Alternative Explanations." *American Economic Review* 82 (3): 371–391.

Bureau of Economic Analysis. 1999. *Regional Economic Information System, 1969–1998.* CD-ROM. Washington, D.C.: U.S. Department of Commerce, Bureau of Economic Analysis.

Bureau of Economic Analysis. 2000. *Historical Personal Income for States, 1929–1957.* Washington, D.C.: U.S. Department of Commerce, Bureau of Economic Analysis. Available on-line at http://www.bea.doc.gov/bea/regional/spi.

Bureau of Labor Statistics. 1978–1998a. "Civilians at Work by Sex, Age, Race, Hispanic Origin, and Hours of Work," or similarly titled tables. *Geographic Profile of Employment and Unemployment.* Annual. Washington, D.C.: U.S. Department of Labor, Bureau of Labor Statistics.

Bureau of Labor Statistics. 1978–1998b. "Civilians at Work 1 to 34 Hours by Sex, Race, Reason for Working Less Than 35 Hours and Usual Status," or similarly titled tables. *Geographic Profile of Employment and Unemployment.* Annual. Washington, D.C.: U.S. Department of Labor, Bureau of Labor Statistics.

Bureau of Labor Statistics. 1999a. "Average Hours and Earnings of Production or Nonsupervisory Workers on Private Nonfarm Payrolls by Major Industry, 1964 to Date." Table B-2. *Employment and Earnings* 46 (8): 47.

Bureau of Labor Statistics. 1999b. "Multiple Job Holding, by State." *Monthly Labor Review* 122 (6): 39.

Bureau of Labor Statistics. 2000a. Local Area Unemployment Statistics. Available on-line at http://stats.bls.gov/lauhome.htm.

Bureau of Labor Statistics. 2000b. "Persons at Work in Agriculture and Nonagricultural Industries by Hours of Work." Table A-23. *Employment and Earnings* 47 (4): 24.

Bureau of Labor Statistics. 2000c. "Persons at Work in All and Nonagricultural Industries by Reason for Working Less Than 35 Hours and Usual Full- or Part-Time Status." Table A-24. *Employment and Earnings* 47 (4): 24.

Ciccone, Antonio, and Robert E. Hall. 1996. "Productivity and the Density of Economic Activity." *American Economic Review* 86 (1): 54–70.

Cromartie, John B. 1998. "Net Migration in the Great Plains Increasingly Linked to Natural Amenities and Suburbanization." *Rural Development Perspectives* 13 (1): 27–34.

Cromartie, John B., and John M. Wardwell. 1999. "Migrants Settling Far and Wide in the Rural West." *Rural Development Perspectives* 14 (2): 2–8.

Denison, Edward F. 1974. *Accounting for United States Economic Growth, 1929–1969.* Washington, D.C.: Brookings Institution.

Denison, Edward F. 1985. *Trends in American Economic Growth, 1929–1982.* Washington, D.C.: Brookings Institution.

Devlin, Sherry. 2000a. "Economic Impact Being Hotly Debated." *Missoulian* (Missoula, Mont.), June 18.

Devlin, Sherry. 2000b. "Fighting for Their West." *Missoulian* (Missoula, Mont.), July 3.

DiNardo, John, Nicole M. Fortin, and Thomas Lemieux. 1996. "Labor Market Institutions and the Distribution of Wages, 1973–1992: A Semiparametric Approach." *Econometrica* 64 (5): 1001–1044.

Echeverria, John D., and Raymond Booth Eby. 1995. *Let the People Judge: Wise Use and the Private Property Rights Movement.* Washington, D.C.: Island Press.

Eller, T. J. 1996. *Who Stays Poor? Who Doesn't?* Current Population Report No. P70-55. Washington, D.C.: U.S. Department of Commerce, U.S. Census Bureau.

Evans, Alan W. 1990. "The Assumption of Equilibrium in the Analysis of Migration and Interregional Differences: A Review of Some Recent Research." *Journal of Regional Science* 30 (4): 515–531.

Filer, Randall K., Daniel S. Hamermesh, and Albert E. Rees. 1996. *The Economics of Work and Pay.* 6th ed. New York: HarperCollins College Publishers.

Fortin, Nicole M., and Thomas Lemieux. 1997. "Institutional Change and Rising Wage Inequality: Is There a Linkage?" *Journal of Economic Perspectives* 11 (2): 75–96.

Freeman, A. Myrick. 1993. *The Measurement of Environmental and Resource Values: Theory and Methods.* Washington, D.C.: Resources for the Future.

Goodstein, Eban S. 1999. *Economics and the Environment.* 2nd ed. Upper Saddle River, N.J.: Prentice-Hall.

Gottschalk, Peter. 1997. "Inequality, Income Growth, and Mobility: The Basic Facts." *Journal of Economic Perspectives* 11 (2): 21–40.

Gottschalk, Peter, and Sheldon Danziger. 1997. *Family Income Mobility: How Much Is There and Has It Changed?* Working Paper No. 398. Chestnut Hill, Mass.: Boston College, Department of Economics.

Greenwood, Michael J., G. L. Hunt, D. S. Rickman, and G. I. Treyz. 1991. "Migration, Regional Equilibrium, and the Estimation of Compensating Differentials." *American Economic Review* 81 (5): 1382–1390.

Grose, Andrew P. 1995. *The West on a Slippery Slope: High Growth, Low Pay.* San Francisco: WESTRENDS, The Council of State Governments.

Harrigan, Frank J., and Peter G. McGregor. 1993. "Equilibrium and Disequilibrium Perspectives on Regional Labor Migration." *Journal of Regional Science* 33 (1): 49–67.

Haveman, Robert H. 1996. *Earnings Inequality: The Influence of Changing Opportunities and Choices.* Washington, D.C.: American Enterprise Institute.

Jamison, Michael. 2000a. "Anti-government Fervor to Spill into Libby Streets." *Missoulian* (Missoula, Mont.), March 15.

Jamison, Michael. 2000b. "Talking from the Trenches." *Missoulian* (Missoula, Mont.), January 21.

Juhn, Chinhui, Kevin M. Murphy, and Brooks Pierce. 1993. "Wage Inequality and the Rise in Returns to Skill." *Journal of Political Economy* 101 (3): 410–442.

Kelinson, Jonathan W., and Patricia Tate. 2000. "The 1998–2008 Job Outlook in Brief." *Occupational Outlook Quarterly* 44 (1): 2–39.

Krueger, Alan. B., and Lawrence H. Summers. 1986. "Reflections on the Inter-Industry Wage Structure." In *Unemployment and the Structure of Labor Markets*, edited by K. Lang and J. Leonard. London: Basil Blackwell.

Krueger, Alan. B., and Lawrence H. Summers. 1988. "Efficiency Wages and the Inter-Industry Wage Structure." *Econometrica* 56 (2): 259–293.

Krugman, Paul R., and Maurice Obstfeld. 1997. *International Economics: Theory and Policy*. 4th ed. Reading, Mass.: Addison-Wesley.

Lee, Chulhee. 2000. "The Relation of the Growth in Income Inequality to the Organization of Work and the Structure of Consumption." App. 5E in *The Fourth Great Awakening and the Future of Egalitarianism,* edited by Robert William Fogel. Chicago: University of Chicago Press.

Long, Larry H., and Kristin A. Hansen. 1975. "Trends in Return Migration to the South." *Demography* 12 (November): 601–614.

McGinnis, Wendy J., Ervin G. Schuster, and Walter L. Stewart. 1996. *Economic Indicator Maps for Rural Development in the Pacific West*. Intermountain Research Station General Technical Report No. INT-GTR-328. Ogden, Utah: U.S. Department of Agriculture, Forest Service, Intermountain Research Station.

McGrattan, Ellen R., and Richard Rogerson. 1998. "Changes in Hours Worked since 1950." Federal Reserve Bank of Minneapolis *Quarterly Review* 22 (1): 2–19.

Marston, Ed. 1996. "Denying the Warts on the West's Service Economy." *High Country News* 28 (24): 14–15.

Marston, Ed. 1999. Reviewer's response to letter to the editor by Thomas M. Power, "Do Low Incomes Make Montana 'Poor'?" *High Country News* 31 (14): 11.

Marston, Stephen T. 1985. "Two Views of the Geographic Distribution of Unemployment." *Quarterly Journal of Economics* 100 (1): 57–78.

Mills, Edwin S., and Bruce W. Hamilton. 1989. *Urban Economics*. 4th ed. Boston: Scott, Foresman.

Mishel, Lawrence, Jared Bernstein, and John Schmitt. 1996. *The State of Working America, 1996–1997*. Washington, D.C.: Economic Policy Institute.

Missoulian. 1999. Editorial, *Missoulian* (Missoula, Mont.), November 11.

Montana Department of Labor and Industry. 1999. *Profile of the Montana Worker Data Supplement*. Helena: Montana Department of Labor and Industry.

Murphy, Kevin M., and Finis Welch. 1993. "Industrial Change and the Rising Importance of Skill." In *Uneven Tides: Rising Inequality in America*, edited by Sheldon Danziger and Peter Gottschalk. New York: Russell Sage Foundation.

Naifeh, Mary. 1998. *Trap Door? Revolving Door? Or Both?* Current Population Report No. P70-63. Washington, D.C.: U.S. Department of Commerce, U.S. Census Bureau.

National Technical Information Center. 1997. *North American Industry Classification System (NAICS)—United States*. Springfield, Va.: National Technical Information Center. Parts of report available on-line at http://www.census.gov/epcd/www/naics.html.

Nelson, Peter B. 1999. "Quality of Life, Nontraditional Income, and Economic Growth: New Development Opportunities for the Rural West." *Rural Development Perspectives* 14 (2): 32–37.

Oaxaca, Ronald. 1973. "Male–Female Differentials in Urban Labor Markets." *International Economic Review* 14 (3): 693–709.

Office of Management and Budget. 1987. *Standard Industrial Classification Manual, 1987*. Washington, D.C.: Office of Management and Budget.

O'Sullivan, Arthur. 1993. *Urban Economics*. 2nd ed. Homewood, Ill.: Irwin.

Pendley, William Perry. 1995. *War on the West*. Washington, D.C.: Regnery Publishing.

Power, Thomas M. 1980. *The Economic Value of the Quality of Life*. Boulder, Colo.: Westview Press.

Power, Thomas M. 1998. "'Where Have All the School Children Gone?' Are Low Wages and High Costs of Living Driving Young Families from Montana?" Unpublished research report. Missoula: University of Montana, Department of Economics.

Rathge, Richard, and Paula Highman. 1998. "Population Change in the Great Plains: A History of Prolonged Decline." *Rural Development Perspectives* 13 (1): 19–25.

Roback, Jennifer. 1982. "Wages, Rents, and the Quality of Life." *Journal of Political Economy* 90 (6): 1257–1277.

Roback, Jennifer. 1988. "Wages, Rents, and Amenities: Differences among Workers and Regions." *Economic Inquiry* 26 (1): 23–41.

Robinson, J. P., and G. Godbey. 1997. Chap. 5 in *Time for Life: The Surprising Ways Americans Use Their Time*. University Park: Pennsylvania State University Press.

Robison, M. Henry, Charles W. McKetta, and Steven S. Peterson. 1996. *A Study of the Effects of Changing Federal Timber Policies on Rural Communities in Northcental Idaho*. Moscow: University of Idaho.

Rones, Phillip L., Randy E. Ilg, and Jennifer M. Gardner. 1997. "Trends in Hours of Work since the Mid-1970s." *Monthly Labor Review* 120 (4): 3–14.

Rowley, Thomas D. 1998. "Sustaining the Great Plains." *Rural Development Perspectives* 13 (1): 2–6.

Rudzitis, Gundars. 1999. "Amenities Increasingly Draw People to the Rural West." *Rural Development Perspectives* 14 (2): 9–13.

Schor, Juliet B. 1991. *The Overworked American: The Unexpected Decline of Leisure*. New York: Basic Books.

Shaffer, Ron. 1989. *Community Economics*. Ames: Iowa State University Press.

Shea, Martina. 1995. *Poverty, 1991–1993*. Current Population Report No. P70-45. Washington, D.C.: U.S. Department of Commerce, U.S. Census Bureau.

Stegner, Wallace. 1980. *The Sound of Mountain Water: The Changing American West*. 1969. Reprint, New York: Penguin Putnam.

Stuart, David E. 2000. *Anasazi America*. Albuquerque: University of New Mexico Press.

Templeton, Neil. 1998. "Analysis of Movement in Real and Relative Wages in the Pacific Northwest from 1977 to 1993." Master's thesis, University of Montana, Department of Economics.

Toole, Ken. 1997. "How the Far Right Spreads Its 'Wacky' Ideas." *High Country News* 29 (23): 12–13.

U.S. Census Bureau. 1983. *County and City Data Book, 1983*. Washington, D.C.: U.S.

Department of Commerce, U.S. Census Bureau.

U.S. Census Bureau. 1999a. *Historical Annual Time Series of State Population Estimates and Demographic Components of Change: 1900 to 1990 Total Population Estimates.* Available on-line at http://www.census.gov/population/www/estimates/st_stts.html.

U.S. Census Bureau. 1999b. *Statistical Abstract of the United States: 1999.* Annual; 119th ed. Washington, D.C.: U.S. Department of Commerce, U.S. Census Bureau.

U.S. Census Bureau. 2000a. *State Population Estimates and Demographic Components of Population Change: April 1, 1990, to July 1, 1999.* Available on-line at http://www.census.gov/population/estimates/state/st-99-2.txt.

U.S. Census Bureau. 2000b. *State Rankings of Population Change and Demographic Components of Population Change for the Period July 1, 1998, to July 1, 1999.* Available on-line at http://www.census.gov/population/estimates/state/st-99-4.txt.

U.S. Department of Agriculture. 1997. "Employment Growth and Unemployment Rate Often Identify Different Counties as Prosperous." *Rural Conditions and Trends* 8 (2): 14–17.

U.S. Department of Agriculture. 1998a. *1997 Census of Agriculture Highlights.* Available on-line at http://www.nass.usda.gov/census/census97/highlights/ag-state.htm.

U.S. Department of Agriculture. 1998b. "Nonmetro Population Growth Rebound of the 1990s Continues, but at a Slower Recent Rate." *Rural Trends and Conditions* 8 (2): 46–59.

Valletta, Robert G. 1997. "Effects of Industry Employment Shifts on U.S. Wage Structure." Federal Reserve Bank of San Francisco *Economic Review* 1:16–32.

Vias, Alexander C. 1999. "Jobs Follow People in the Rural Rocky Mountain West." *Rural Development Perspectives* 14 (2): 24–31.

Voith, Richard. 1991. "Capitalization of Local and Regional Attributes into Wages and Rents: Differences across Residential, Commercial, and Mixed-Use Communities." *Journal of Regional Science* 31 (2): 127–145.

von Reichert, Christiane. 1998. "Who Are the Migrants and Why Do They Come? Analysis of Survey Data Focusing on Return and New Migrants to Montana." Unpublished research report. Missoula: University of Montana, Department of Geography.

Widenor, Marcus. 1991. "Pattern Bargaining in the Pacific Northwest Lumber and Sawmill Industry: 1980–1989." In *Labor in a Global Economy: Perspectives from the U.S. and Canada*, edited by S. Hecker and M. Hallock. Eugene: University of Oregon, Labor Education and Research Center.

Wilson, William Julius. 1987. *The Truly Disadvantaged: The Inner City, the Underclass, and Public Policy.* Chicago: University of Chicago Press.

Wilson, William Julius. 1997. *When Work Disappears: The World of the New Urban Poor.* Chicago: University of Chicago Press.

About the Authors

RICHARD N. BARRETT is a professor of economics at the University of Montana. He received his Ph.D. degree from the University of Wisconsin at Madison. He previously edited *International Dimensions of the Environmental Crisis* (Boulder, Colo.: Westview Press, 1982).

THOMAS MICHAEL POWER is a professor of economics and chairman of the Department of Economics at the University of Montana. He received his Ph.D. degree from Princeton University. He is the author of *Lost Landscapes and Failed Economies: The Search for a Value of Place* (Washington, D.C.: Island Press, 1996); *Environmental Protection and Economic Well-Being: The Economic Pursuit of Quality* (Armonk, N.Y.: M. E. Sharpe, 1996); *The Economic Pursuit of Quality* (Armonk, N.Y.: M. E. Sharpe, 1988); and *The Economic Value of the Quality of Life* (Boulder, Colo.: Westview Press, 1980).

Index

ISLAND PRESS BOARD OF DIRECTORS

Chair
HENRY REATH
President, Collector's Reprints, Inc.

Vice-Chair
VICTOR M. SHER
Environmental Lawyer

Secretary
DANE NICHOLS
Chairman, The Natural Step, U.S.

Treasurer
DRUMMOND PIKE
President, The Tides Foundation

WILLIAM M. BACKER
Backer, Spielvogel, Bates (ret.)

ROBERT E. BAENSCH
Professor of Publishing,
New York University

MABEL H. CABOT

DAVID C. COLE
Sunnyside Farms, LLC

CATHERINE M. CONOVER

GENE E. LIKENS
Director,
The Institute of Ecosystem Studies

CAROLYN PEACHEY
Campbell Peachey & Associates

WILL ROGERS
Trust for Public Lands

CHARLES C. SAVITT
President, Center for Resource
Economics/Island Press

SUSAN E. SECHLER
Director of Global Programs,
The Rockefeller Foundation

PETER R. STEIN
Managing Partner, The Lyme
Timber Company

RICHARD TRUDELL
Executive Director, American
Indian Resources Institute

WREN WIRTH
President,
The Winslow Foundation